Walking with the Bear

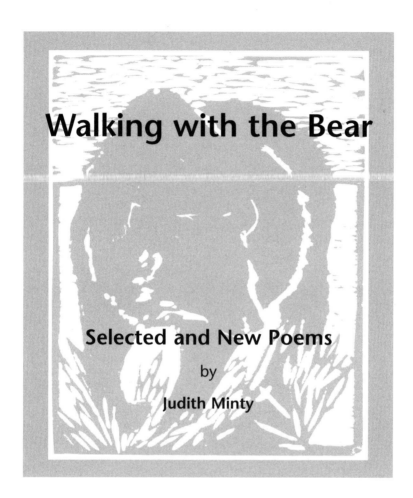

Walking with the Bear

Selected and New Poems

by

Judith Minty

Michigan State University Press
East Lansing

∞The paper used in this publication meets the minimum requirements of ANSI/NISO Z39.48–1992 (R 1997) (Permanence of Paper).

Michigan State University Press
East Lansing, Michigan 48823-5202

Printed and Bound in the United States of America

04 03 02 01 00   1 2 3 4 5

LIBRARY OF CONGRESS CATALOGING-IN-PUBLICATION DATA

Minty, Judith
    Walking with the bear: selected and new poems / by Judith Minty.
    p.   cm.
    ISBN 0-87013-547-3 (alk. paper)
    I. Title.
    PS3563.I48 W35 2000
    811'.54—dc21
                                                         99-050948

Acknowledgments:
Poems have been selected from the following books and chapbooks:
Lake Songs and Other Fears (Pittsburgh, Penn.: University of Pittsburgh Press, 1974); *In the Presence of Mothers* (Pittsburgh, Penn.: University of Pittsburgh Press, 1981); *Yellow Dog Journal* (Los Angeles, Calif.: Center Publications, 1979) (rpt. Berkeley, Calif.: Parallax Press, 1991); *Letters to My Daughters* (Ann Arbor, Mich.: Mayapple Press, 1980); *Counting the Losses* (Aptos, Calif.: Jazz Press, 1986); *Dancing the Fault* (Gainesville, Fla.: University Press of Florida, 1991).

The editors of the following magazines and anthologies in which some of the new poems appeared in slightly different form are gratefully acknowledged:
"Alone at Prairie Creek" and "Sleepwalkers" in *LUNA;* "Walking with the Bear" in *Woman Poet: The Midwest;* "Deer at the Door" and "First Snow" in *Controlled Burn;* "Destroying the Cormorant Eggs" in *South Coast Poetry Journal;* "The Language of Whales" in *Poems for the Wild Earth;* "October Light" and "At Manitoulin" in *New Poems from the Third Coast;* "Snow Geese Over Lincoln, Nebraska" in *The Bloomsbury Review;* "Recognizing" in *ICE-FLOE;* "Walking the Beach in Fog" in *Redstart.*

Cover art is a woodcut entitled "Minty's Bear" by Anne Larson Hollerbach
Cover design by Heidi Dailey
Book design by Michael J. Brooks

Visit Michigan State University Press on the World Wide Web
        www.msu.edu/unit/msupress

to Ed

Contents

New Poems

from *Lake Songs and Other Fears*

Those grand fresh-water seas of ours—Erie, and Ontario, and Huron, and Superior, and Michigan . . . they know what shipwrecks are, for out of sight of land, they have drowned full many a midnight ship with all its shrieking crew.

—Herman Melville

Leland

Robert says it reminds him of Scotland
the way waves spume over the seawall
into the still harbor and the bluff
looms black and ominous above. He rode
a gray horse once over the rolling hills
of the peninsula. "Like moors," he said.
"Like home. I was a child again."

On the beach I found a dead seagull,
feathers like fur, so white
they seemed brushstrokes on canvas.
All afternoon I sat with the gull,
let waves rock us back and forth,
watched his outstretched neck, his beak
biting into the sand, his last hold on earth.

The Fourth of July Drowning

They came for you, fumbling through fog,
the half-men, hunchbacked in black suits.
They searched for the echo of your cry,
for your shadow, for your hair floating up
like blind spider legs reaching for light.
Sunless they groped, fins pushing deeper.

Now under siren, through fog
and waves, they bring you to port
hunched, knees drawn up to your chin,
the black bag warm like new beginnings.
Tall women wait cold in the crowd,
their arms closed and empty now.

The Island

—for Ronald Riker

The snakegrass curled on my desk
begins to yellow at the joints.
Withered, it looks more alive
than when I stole it from South Manitou—
that thieving island that swallows
inward in circles to deserted lighthouse,
to the Rikers who live there alone
without a son, to the cry of obsessed gulls.
In this curling heat I put together
the segments, quickly before fear starts.

Lake Michigan

This lake is cruel.
I drowned here when I was ten,
slid into this water that runs
up the little finger,
felt arms cradle me, no longer
cried for mother, was sucked into black sleep.

This lake chews at dunes,
bites off chunks of sand,
then ebbs back
as firs lean and topple, their roots
dragging deeper roots
until cellars, kitchens, toilets collapse.

Gulls scream at it
from their rookery, then scatter
to tap-dance on ice floes
in January thaws. In June
they fold their wings back
for long suicide dives.

This lake has a memory. It knows
the fingerprints of my cry.
I strip off my clothes,
fall into the waves. I will
go deep, let it lick my skin,
feel its pulse as we sink again together.

Homage to Mister Bones

385 dreams
     spun round
in that dog-
tired head,
all searching for the door
     the exit
     whirling
to escape.
Minnesota's dawn
hung cold
     almost
like Breughel's landscape.
From the bridge
for a moment
     Henry fancied
he saw three hunters
in the snow and
raised his hand
     knowing.

     Whirl
and rejoice
from the harbor's
dark floor.
     We
do you glory. See!
Three birds watch;
     the fourth flies.

Canada Goose

The goose has been living
on our lake for a week. When feet
snap dry leaves, she scuttles,
blankets herself in reeds.

We peer out from shore,
try to tempt her with grain, but she
blends gray feathers, black head
in sheets of shadow and water.

Each fall I wait for them
to come honking, for those great V's
that point south. I want to see
them homing, farther than I can go.

The old ones say wild geese live
thirty years, mate for life.
Now she starts her long wait
alone in the first snowfall.

The Horse in the Meadow

I saw him, that wild stallion,
when I dressed in white. He galloped
along our ridge at dusk,
ran against the sky's flame,
mane and tail streaming fine strands.

Here, he grazes in the meadow
where birds sing yellow songs,
where the wind blows in circles.
Coat damp, glistening, his flanks
burn as he paws at grass
and listens for thunder.

She is dressed in black, that old crone.
She leans on the fence, cooing,
reaches out with bony hand
and offers him sweets.
I know her. She wants to
touch those velvet ears, run hands

over that strong back, braid her fingers
in that mane. She wants to
climb on him, break him,
ride him back to her house. She
wants to hobble him, rein him.
She wants to hide him in her bed at night.

If I let her, there will be
no color from birds' mouths,
no lightning in clouds.
There will be no more girls
dreaming in sheets of fire.

The Cats in the Barn

"Diese Katzen be killers!"
The chicken dead
and the cats still there
in the fray of feathers and clucking.
And Herr Muller bellowing,
the gunnysack already in his hand.
Those hands,
weathered from milking cows
and counting hens' eggs
in countless half-dawns,
the knuckle creases lined
with soil from his potato field.
His fury making even his blond
mustache tremble; those hands
grabbing at the cats by the neck
legs tail, stuffing
them into the bag; those
hands that lay gentle on my shoulder
when I came for visits to his barn.
I saw what he was going to do.
The cats mewing, him roaring,
a twelve-year-old girl wanting to run,
but pressed instead against the barn wall.
Those hands banging
the gunnysack against the post,
the cats howling, screeching
in their darkness. The sun
stabbing my eyes, me whispering
to him to stop,
begging the cats to stop crying,
wishing those hands to be still.

The Legacy

No need to dial the doctor. I have
already heard that it flows in the genes,
floats on invisible electric currents
perhaps, from mother to son
to daughter, the mother again.

I have been to that old barn, looked
up through the dusting sunlight
from loft to splintered rafter; have almost
seen the rope, the empty space full with her
sagging skirt and dangling legs.

I have listened, but they never speak
her name, that grandmother
shrouded in dust, the grave
marked with whispers that sin begets sinner.
I have ceased to pray to the Virgin.

No matter. Yesterday I saw fire
in a cat's eye, touched the coarse mane
of a wild horse, at last set my house
in order. At night
clouds form in front of the moon.

Why Do You Keep Those Cats?

All winter, those cats of mine
doze like old women in front of the fire,
curl their fur around saucers of sunlight
they have trapped on the rug. Sometimes
they bury themselves in the wool of blankets
to sniff dreams I left there.

Awake, their eyes reflect deeper sleeps.
Delicate tongues yawn, hide needles of teeth.
I listen for their soft paws,
for their purrs to rattle in slow circles
near my bed. They want to capture
warmth from my body. "Why do you

keep those cats?" my neighbors ask.
Why? It is for summer that I wait
for their claws to unsheathe, for their eyes
to blaze orange in dark hallways.
Soon they will tear at my door, howl
to walk with lions along the fence.

It is not for winter. It is instead
for the flame of yellow moons.
Then I run wild with them,
hide in trees, sleep again in leaves;
in August I will sink my teeth,
as they do, into the warm necks of mice.

Blue Baby

Sister of the congenital heart, meant to be
two years younger than I,
playmate for swings and dolls.
You, Patricia, doll of my parents'
love nights, there was no time—blue death
staining lips and fingertips, creeping
toward the murmur in your nursery crib.

Without you, I grew, whispered to your shadow,
played sister to our dolls—
and saw you often, deep
in the garden of our mother's eyes.
Still I bloomed, forgot you
until my guilt matured: a blue vein
that twists now in the pulse of my heart.

Upon Seeing the Aurora Borealis for the First Time on My 35th Birthday

For me, the birthday girl, it was a portent.
I waited, almost hoping we would never see those lights.
For the others, it was an excursion
like a carnival trip to see freaks expose their anomalies.
I would have liked red wine, a toast,
the Eucharist even. Instead there was
cigarettes and Scotch, the flash of matches and laughter.

Stretched out on cool sand, the sky spilling stars,
we were first-nighters waiting for the curtain.
I thought of my Nordic father, how he had seen that show
birthdays ago up near the Arctic Circle;
the reverence in his voice as he told
how, like an umbrella it had opened perfectly over his head,
the rays fingering down so close he could have touched them.

And then, from over the lake, it began for us.
First a flicker of candles, then a blaze
of white yellow orange. It was
a blossoming: the petals unfurled, stretched
out from the earth in their celebration of beams and arcs;
withering, then brilliance;
silence, then an explosion of light.

It was quiet before terror, before they
began to roll as if alive. I wanted to
shut my eyes, cry out that the umbrella was gone.
Only ghosts now, raining, tumbling, roaring
over each other; years chasing, haunting across the sky.
He said, "I thought the world was coming to an end."
And, Papa, it did then—in a way.

—The Ovals/Lake Michigan

14

Waiting for the Transformation

My daughter is a mystic about cats.
I am afraid. I have seen her conversing with them,
watched her nod, blink her eyes; and the cats
twitch their whiskers, almost smile.
When she was five, she told me that if our old Tom
curled close to the fire, there would be
snow the next day. Often there was.

I think, although I fear to know for certain,
that she becomes a cat at night.
Just yesterday, I saw tiger shadows
on the wall of her room. I hear strange cries
in the house before dawn, feel the shiver of purrs,
a softness that feathers my face.

I do not think about it, tell no one.
I have decided to wait until other children's eyes
glint fire, until they all leave their mothers' arms
and turn wild—howling in the night.

Winter Tree

—for M. H., 1889–1971

I

It is three years since they uprooted you
from your wilting, flowered chair
and that cluttered house
with its fading wallpaper blossoms;
tore your hands from the basement workbench
where you stood planted
on braided rugs thin with years of feet;
since they sold your furniture and dishes,
drove away your car, gave you back
two pipes to smoke and one blue suit for Sundays.

II

For three years you tried to spread out roots
in that gnarled orchard, the Old Folk's Home;
strained to hear the mumbling man next door
and to read each night's microscopic news;
watched the nuns float over you like birds, white feathers
fluttering, voices cooing, faces downed in prayer;
retreated from your neighbors' twisted fingers
and faded eyes; avoided mouths that ate themselves
and minds that listened only to the past;
saw snow turn to rain and back again;
felt leaves wither, branches tremble.

III

Today we stood in the shade of the chapel
and thanked the fumbling priest who forgot your name.
Then we packed your life
in two brown cardboard boxes: pajamas and underwear
leafed with tobacco, a half-eaten box of chocolates,
the gold watch still keeping time.

Oh, Grandpa, Old Man. The tallest tree
is where the eagle builds his nest.

Making Music

Tuesday afternoons in the cave of our basement,
my mother, like an organist,
sat in front of the old white mangle,
her music heaped in a wicker basket beside her.
I saw the flash of fur under her arm

as she lifted a sheet, folded it twice, and with her knee
moved the pedal that made her instrument go.
I watched wrinkles feed into the mangle, heard a hiss
as heat met dampness of muslin, smelled soap under scorch,
saw clean hymns flow out of the roller.

I have no talent for music, am not my mother.
Two hours by car from Kalamazoo to Muskegon
I sit behind the wheel, direct my instrument
along a white line, around curves, over rises;
my pedal maintains a tempo of seventy miles an hour.

Headlights rest on the fur of dead animals, and my wheels
roll over them: rabbits, cats, squirrels
pressed into the sheet of highway. It is a long drive home.
The hum of my motor blends with the thump of bodies
and the static rock beat out of the radio.

from *In the Presence of Mothers*

All of us forever seeking again this warmth and this darkness,
this being alive without pain, this being alive without anxiety
or fear or aloneness.

—*Anaïs Nin*

Palmistry for Blind Mariners

1. The Dunes
The hand: an island surrounded by oceans,
five sisters joined in a circle.
Past this desert of shifting sand, green
gropes for roots in the cup of the palm.
Forget the thumb. It's on the other side
and we dare not chart that course yet
through those reefs of birth and death.

Even here, close to shore, we're in danger.
The lake curls its tongue
round the point and the land strikes
back. Tree stumps spear at our hull
and wolves howl gale warnings.
When the wind shifts, let out the chute.
Run with it, head North for open water.

2. Heart Line
This channel is long, sounds fathoms
deep, a river that runs
through Muskegon, Grand Rapids, Lansing,
forks off toward Detroit.
But those narrows are death and we cannot
cruise them for, oh sailors,
there are so many here to love.
Stay. Drop anchor. Drift back with the current.

Let the stream wash
over years as it slices your wrist.
Feel the chill of empty rooms change
as hands burn your body and blankets
cocoon around skin
that beads with the fear of new knowledge.

Cry out the old pain,
the breaking, the separating, move on
as whispers tremble to banks.

Touch willow branches with fingertips.
Swim after trout.
Listen for laughter. It is there in the night
fires, the call of cats, in the eagle's wing
when he hunkers down from the sun.
Weave water lilies into garlands and give them
as gifts. Gather stones for your house.
Live here always, if you can.

3. The North Woods
Summer passes too quickly.
Winter brings pain. The past
dries like strawflowers.
We must change camp before withering
begins. In this Indian summer
the sun lowers its flame
over the lake, ignites
on flint stone of the Chippewa fathers.

Our canoe is ready, stripped bark
from birch trees. We will travel light,
eat berries and roots
along the way, leave footprints in sand.
Deer will drink from our hands
and the hoot of owls will guide us.
But I warn you, there will be
wailing and a beating of breasts.

Dip your paddle as you pass the bear,
asleep at the foot of her dune,
who mourns cubs, lost
in the crossing from Wisconsin.
Forget love rites and matings
and children. Bury them
deep under Mercury's mound.
This lake and mothers are cruel.

Hold close to the calm
of fingers, pass gulls who curse
from their rookery.
Let fog cling like webs
to your face, your hair. Glide
into whispers of vapor.
Grope for land if you wish. Go ashore
if you are tired of seafaring.

For my part, I know this hand
and cannot turn in again.
If you must, follow me. I am going
past the islands out
into the lake. There is a place
I have heard of where you can sink
deep into the center of dreams, where waves
will rock you in sleep, where everything
is as you wished it to be.

Finding a Depth

I

These North Channel islands are forgotten children
of the glacier. Some sink
in beards of grass.
Others, like oases, sprout umbrella trees out of rock.
Clusters, buds in the center of water.
So many, so alike that each, heavily-wooded,
each, stony-beached, becomes the other.

At a family reunion when I was a child,
I remember being spun,
groping to find cousins and brother
in the dark behind my blindfold,
crying when I stood alone in the field.

II

The beach is so rocky I must
wear shoes for protection. Stones
clatter and crawl under my feet. White and flat,
they blend like a big Irish family.

I bend, pick one up, and flicking my wrist
send it out over the lake.
Another and another.
I am not very adept at this game. Still
one comes alive and with five
great, slanting skips goes far before sinking.

III

In this cove, with only this boat
anchored in the sunlight, I sit facing reeds.
The Channel beach at my back is piled
with white, flat stones.

I have been watching a beaver glide in and out
of shadow. It occurs to me
that a person, if she wanted, could disappear here,
name and position lost
like a misplaced photo from an album,
the loss felt here, in the chest,
a flat sinking into self.

—North Channel/Lake Huron

In Fire

1.

They are burning the tree
in the vacant lot. Flames
circle its legs, lick at dry leaves
until they bend, powder to ashes.
The tree's roots
run deep; a martyr,
its branches reach out. In the field
the only sound is crackling fire.

2.

Saint Joan tied to the stake,
all white. Lilies
stretch over the field
like her virgin banner blazing in the sun.
But the punishment is for listening
to voices. The greatest vision
comes in that last echo
of unbearable heat.

3.

The old crazy woman, hidden away
in the house next door.
Her face wavers
against windows as, wild-eyed,
she twists her mouth to tell children
visions. Witch, we hear her
scream through the heat of summer nights
and shut our eyes, smiling.

4.

All gone, all gone. Fire
consumes us as we spread out
our arms, let flesh curl from the bones.
But roots burn slowly
and we see white visions in the flame.
Crumbling, bending to the pain, we
open our mouths, speak finally,
never know if our voice is heard.

The Lake Road

We drive along the lake road
toward water, the sky
so blue the two will blend together
at the horizon. We may never know
whether we sink or fly.

The talk is of breaking
through heat into waves, crashing
against foam. Father mother children, we will
flutter, stroke, spread out our arms,
float in again to shore.

We did not intend the splash of orange
at the road's edge, a family
of orioles scattered on the grass, broken
when they lifted, fell
in and out of currents.

The sun breaks its wings
against our windshield. On fire, we soar
over the rise to the lake.

The End of Summer

1.

The old bitch labrador swims
in heavy circles. Under water
her legs run free without their limp.
She stretches brown eyes toward me,
snorting, and the stick I throw
stirs gray memories of ten Octobers,
ducks that fly at the sun and fall.

2.

On the Pere Marquette River, salmon
quiver upstream from the lake, return
to alpha. At the dam
they leap and throw themselves
through currents, stretch
and spend themselves
against the torrent from the falls.

3.

All week the sky has filled
with orange petals. Butterflies
floating in cycles toward milkweed,
monarchs freed from their chrysalis,
waiting for the wind's current
to die. The beach
is covered with torn wings.

4.
Fire, off the merganser's hood.
This summer he nested
in our channel, drifted
with the half-tame mallards. His sharp bill
stabs water to catch bread I throw.
But he belongs by the sea. I want him
to fly now, before October and guns.

Prowling the Ridge

You, husband, lying next to
me in our bed, growl
like a wild dog or wolf
as you travel the woods
of your dream.
I feel your legs running
from or after some

thing. Now you turn
and curl toward the moon.
Away from me, you
prowl along ridges, hunt
with the pack. You rest
your paws on wild fur, bare
teeth to raw meat.

If I reach out and touch
the curve of your haunch,
brush my hand over your skin,
I can tame you
back to this room, to this wife
still outside
your blanket of sleep.

But it's your dream
I burn for, the other
place and time.
Wolf, leave tracks now. Quick.
Let me follow your scent.

Conjoined

a marriage poem

The onion in my cupboard, a monster, actually
two joined under one transparent skin:
each half-round, then flat and deformed
where it pressed and grew against the other.

An accident, like the two-headed calf rooted
in one body, fighting to suck at its mother's teats;
or like those other freaks, Chang and Eng, twins
joined at the chest by skin and muscle, doomed
to live, even make love, together for sixty years.

Do you feel the skin that binds us
together as we move, heavy in this house?
To sever the muscle could free one,
but might kill the other. Ah, but men
don't slice onions in the kitchen, seldom see
what is invisible. We cannot escape each other.

Driving East

Floating long hours over the surface
of things, the mind
drifts to fields and branches beyond.
Our car noses over bridges, past
nests of houses, cattle planted at the fence.
Shuddering against headwinds
we almost forget
how it was to walk on land.

When the wind rushes by
in a thunder of feathers, I am struck
suddenly, that we are frail as birds.
Wings snapping
as they brush against trees,
breast crushed on pavement,
the soft fontanel pierced by a stone.

If the oncoming car should veer,
if he should press his foot hard
onto the pedal, if I
should permit my hands to lift off the wheel,
all motion would cease.
Your face broken
against the window, our bones
bent in strange positions of flight.

For Joseph, Who Wrote a Poem about Wild Strawberries

This morning, wild raspberries for breakfast
picked by my daughter and her friend.
One girl is blonde, the other brunette, each
small-breasted, with hips beginning to round.

While I was still uncurling, they bent
at the edge of the woods
and pulled tiny buds from their stems.
A whole pan of them.
Each berry released, suddenly become a cup
and their lips stained, their mouths
puckered from the sweet,
from the sour of the juice.

A month ago, one evening at the beach,
an empty stretch on Lake Michigan,
these girls flung their clothes on the sand
and dropped shyly into waves.
The lake was rough, tossed them
back again. And they, not yet tame,
screamed and fought, then coyly limp,
let the water take them.

As they ran toward me at sunset, I saw
how ripe they were, their skin patched by tans
made in bathing suits, the dark
shadows where their legs sprouted,
the tiny buds of their breasts. And I was ashamed
of my own body, still wrapped in cloth.

You, Joseph, write about wild strawberries becoming art
and that, I suppose, is a part of this poem too.
After breakfast today, we walked to the edge
of the woods, my daughter, her friend,
and I: three women who know about gathering.

The bushes were so plain,
thorny and clogged with spider webs,
the veined leaves not even spectacular.
In a few days the raspberries will be gone
and the plants will look like scrub
to anyone who doesn't know.
But this morning I poured milk
over the berries, watched it purple
in the bottom of my bowl.

Black Bear

Bears make love to women alone by the sea.
                            —Robert Bly

Looming up from old dreams, a hundred
black shapes
of honey lovers, of clumsy dancers
in coats that ripple too large,
of peanut beggars who lift paws behind zoo fences.

More than a dozen times he has
roamed the corners of my yard, reared up, charged.
Sometimes I save children, often myself,
but always I wake
with sweat warm on my palms, fear rising off the bed.

Alone in the woods.
Copper country, my shoes turn rusty after an hour.
A wrong path. I go deeper,
but never reach the lake, though it rises
twice through trees and I smell the waves.

Coming out, a branch cracks. His black head
sinks in the brush. Fur lifts on my neck
and I stir, waking. A stick, three stones, my knife.
I stammer upwind past the burned-out tree stumps,
past his prints in the mud.

Long winters he sleeps. This spring
I stand at the edge and wait.
He growls. I step closer. A shadow rears up.
So we face each other, our breath heaving.
—It is never easy.

Raven

He has set his seal upon my face.
—Posuit Signum

I

For three days his shrieks
ripped through the woods. And I,
not knowing what or who, would miss a step
in the cabin, still my cup
between table and lips.

Things turn when you're alone.
Smoke doesn't rise, trees walk at night.
Sometimes the mind twists into grotesque shapes.

On Thursday then, in a gash
above the falls, his shadow crossed the river
and he opened his throat to me.
I held myself in his dark circle,
was caught by the thrust of his beak.

II

Child in veil and white dress, a taking in.
The wafer melts on my tongue.
Later, other sacraments.
Words spill from my mouth, but they twist,
grow ragged, scatter like feathers.

Now that he has found where I live, he will always
be here. I creep under his wings
and he follows, ruffling robes, reciting matins.

If I open the door, he will perhaps
swoop down and enter, this box
of a house the place of anointment.
Kneeling, lips to the river's curtain,
I begin the ablution, the crossing over.

Winter Poem/The Snowy Owl

1. The Dream/The Need
White on white, it feathers
in layers,
silk folding over silk.
No detail, but the sense
of snow
exploding out of snow.

The sleeper floats within
the dream. White sound
soars from the gaping "O"
of the mouth, all motion
held beyond the outstretched arm
that rises, the cry
sinking into the pillow,
the sheet fluttering,
a cloud against bones.

Blink of yellow light, breath
suspended.
Wings falter, it falls.
The eye
opens, the head revolves,
stares into winter.

2. The Cold/The Motion
This will be their hardest season.
Wind slants, beats snow in circles,
heaves drifts against the house.
She whimpers, but holds the weight and bears
witness to trees bending, to a lake
that sinks into armor. What was
descends. The surface freezes.

She spins inward in the lamplight,
spreads hands over the flame, and speaks
of flight, of something like a cloud
floating over the tundra. Her eyes slit,
round. She tells him she loves him,
though she no longer believes in words.
Tiny animals skitter, become what is hunted.

3. The Hunt/The Pattern
Waiting is the backbone of winter.
Pale light from sun and moon. Cold
whips at skirts, the entrance to sleeves.
Days whirl by without shadow.
She leans into the lash, it coils around her.

Flutter of white by the river. She reels
through drifts like a derelict.
Not him, only snow on a log.
Here, dark things define themselves:
bridge, bare willows lacing the bank,
stump locked in ice near lowland.

It was a mistake to speak of poems
and white owls in a breath, foolish
to count on patterns for a cure, on feathers
that might be gathered off the snow,
ghosts of words waiting to be written.
She returns without him.

4. The Light/The Presence

He comes when she least expects him,
like a lover, out of night into morning.
When he flies by her window, she thinks she hears thunder
and claps her hands to her face. She does not see
his shadow melt into the snow.

He waits in the corner of her garden.
She trembles on the threshold, unable
to go there, to step inside his wings.

White on white, feathers like silk,
the head turns slowly. In winter
dreams hide beneath blankets, only the eyelids glow
yellow chrysanthemums. At last she sees
how fire burns from within and steps forward.
His eyes ignite, the flame rises.

Heights

O human race, born to fly upward,
wherefore at a little wind dost thou so fall?
—Dante

1.
Falling, hanging by my feet
upside down
from the basement stairs.
My mother at the ironing board,
her back turned,
the cry for help
falling from my mouth.
So close
I could almost touch her,
she would not turn.

2.
My friend flew
in the minister's bed, a bird
drifting over ice floes.
He woke when he urinated,
ten years old, ashamed.

3.
When he was a boy
in Muskegon, my husband
climbed Pigeon Hill and jumped,
hovered
before sand thudded up, the grains
fuzzing like down on his skin.

42

That dune is flat now, hauled away
by the boatload and sold.

4.
Another time I stood
at the top of the stairs,
arms spread out,
and stepped off.
Flying is floating,
I did
to the bottom.
No one saw. I never
could do it again.

5.
At Mont Blanc, steps
carved out of ice. Snow
fell all day up there.
We hung skis over our shoulders and clung
to the rope as we climbed,
held ourselves
from looking down the crevasse.

6.
We grow afraid
to speak of it,
forget that we wore capes
once, and leaped
from swings in the backyard.
We close our fists
and fall away.

7.
When the Wallenda pyramid broke,
the family
floated in feathers
to the circus floor.

Karl, the old man, still walks
the cable, sometimes between hotels in Florida.
We tilt our heads back to study the tiny steps,
we whisper
perverse words of flight.

In the Presence of Mothers

1.
Squall lines, laboring,
roll one on the other
out from the island.
Nightmares
out of depths and old drownings,
they rise
with crooning winds,
watery arms.
The breasts of them
weigh against our bones.

2.
Cradled
at the shore's arm,
we fold into the sweet
breath of her hum
and dream
through flashes of light. Her fury
rocks us.

3.
Madonna of the stable,
open the sky to a star
so that we may kneel in the confession box
and cross ourselves with prism points.
Infants become saviors
in their first taste of milk.

4.
In the harbor's barn
our sea-mare
shudders in her stall, flanks
quivering, mast to belly.
Again, *la mer*
calls this horse.
Obedient child, break loose
your reins, ride high over waves, rise
in the trail of her hair.

❧

5.
Black into light and back,
the sun rises and falls in its tedium.
But the delicate stars,
they nurse us
along the moon's yellow path
into hard arms, new openings.

❧

6.
Lovely seasons.
After rain, snow
sails down in tiny boats.
Silence of cold, a falling
of tears. Still,
arms lift out of ice:
the sorrow of it,
the loss.

❧

7.
Back and back, past all
hard rocks and caves, down
into the loam of her skin.
She stirs under the sea
and we enter the way we came,
crying, through cold
to the inner place,
the long warmth of the woman.

Yellow Dog Journal

Fall

> Go, my daughter, to discover
> Why the grey-brown dog is barking,
> And the long-eared dog is baying.
> —Runo XVIII, *Kalevala*

1.
400 miles into north land, driving hard
like a runaway, each town peeling away the woman skin,
turning me pale and soft, as if I
had never married, had not
been planted twenty years in the suburbs.

I come here as my father's child, back
down his rutted road, through a cave of sagging timber
to the clearing. Nothing changed.
His land, his shack leaning over the riverbank,
the Yellow Dog barking home to Superior.

2.
This cabin has not been lived in
since August. October now, and rain
crawls over trees, roof. It muddies the trail.

Bone cold, I light the stove. Damp
shrivels into seams of the walls
and all the flies of summer burst alive again.

They beat their wings against the windows.
They whine and bleat in a confusion of seasons,
then cling to shadows on the ceiling.

I swing at them with a newspaper, wonder
how long I'll last here.
Maple leaves dry yellow on my boots.

3.
My father's slippers, found
in a trunk, now mine to wear.
Too large, creases in the leather
barely touch the flesh.
I slide my toes to the end, along the old ridges.

His feet clump over linoleum floor
table to dishpan, woodbox to stove.
Only the scrap of rug by the door
muffles his presence.

4.
Night comes early in October.
I prop my feet up,
lean into the old rocker.
Rain flows over the roof.
Flames from the wood stove
spin off walls, ceiling,
circle the amber in my glass,
this shack a hive humming.

5.
Last night I drank too much and, almost
asleep, thought of old lovers.
Decided I would hike three miles
to a phone in the morning, call a friend. Ask him
to come north, drive nine hours into autumn.

Today the sky is clear, the trees on fire.
I tie a scarf around my head and walk
to the river for water.

6.
All day, I stay close to the cabin.
My ax rings the morning. And half the afternoon
I gather kindling, spread the sticks
to dry. I am menstruating and have heard
that bear are attracted to women when they bleed.

I haven't spoken in three days, have seen nothing
bigger than chipmunks and squirrels
at the woodpile. It is only beyond the perimeter
that black shapes hide, breath steaming,
low growls circling their throats.
When the branch falls, I swirl to the sound, ax raised.

7.
Sitting on the porch.
Can't tell if I was dozing or reading,
the eye had wandered from words,
turned inward,
so that I only saw it
after the chipmunk's scream.

The hawk spread its wings,
so close I might have touched his feathers,
and lifted the chipmunk up
out of the clearing
and made no sound.

8.
At first, I think they are dogs trailing bear.
I run to the door, that old dream:
copper fur trundling low to my ground,
circling, yelping. The bear
crashing through brush into my clearing,
black coat bristling, eyes burning.

But the clearing is empty. I had forgotten
about geese flying south. Now they bark
across the sky, great packs, sometimes sixty in formation,
silver wingtips over the Yellow Dog,
flowing in and out like white water.
I stand on the porch, dinner fork still in my hand.

9.
The stories that stay with you.
Like Sally's, about the bear
that looked in at her while she was looking out.

This cabin has no curtains.
What's the point,
there are no people here.
But tonight fur rises on my neck
when the bear bawls for Mother and all I see is
an aging woman at my window.

10.
He left this land in the thirties,
left the aunts growing old in Ishpeming,
three sisters without men now
who stir inside the walls of their past.
They want to end where they began,
in the house of their childhood.

He was the oldest brother,
the engineer downstate in Detroit.
Had he stayed, he would have been
a logger, or maybe burst his lungs in the mine.
Summers, he'd cast out for trout,
with no time left for visiting women.

It was he told me the Yellow Dog,
made my sleep spin into the woods, to the falls
above the clearing, the ore shining gold in the sun.
Late nights, he'd whisper its bends,
my face close to his Finnish guttural,
cheeks flushed from his beard's rough stubble.

11.
Beavers gone, but their lodge remains,
broken in the pond. I walk
the edge, sink through twigs and mud,
then circle back to path again. The water
has no motion, like a dream suspended.

Across from me, two birch trees
spring alive in the reflection. They grow out
of clarity. I fall away from the depth of it
and wish someone there to catch me,
to hold me from the roots.

Although I never hear the plane, I catch
its jet stream, born below the birch branches.
It lifts clearly off the surface.
All the way back to the cabin, I
tell myself, "This happened in water."

12.
Thinking how good it is
to come up the path from the river,
chimney smoke sifting above the trees,
to open the cabin door and find myself
still there, stirring logs in the stove.

13.
Crazy. Crazy woman.
      I've stopped combing my hair.
      Now I whisper in the cabin
      and cross myself at dusk.
Crazy. Crazy woman.
      Tonight, on the porch,
      I unbutton my shirt, let my breasts
      swim in the full moon's light.

14.
The raven shrieks.
His shadow cuts the river, west to east,
when I dip my bucket for water.

15.
Now a dog has followed me home.
I hiked three miles north
to the nearest neighbor
to ask if they'd give me wood.
No one home but the beagle puppy.

Tomorrow I'll have to walk
that damned dog back again.
Meanwhile he keeps me warm,
snoring inside my sleeping bag.

16.
Gathering wood today:
rotten logs, twigs, fallen branches.
One knapsack holds six hours of heat,
I mutter, hike
the long trail back
sweating in the afternoon sun.

17.
I miss that beagle. He was spooky
all right, wouldn't stray
more than fifty yards, and scared of the dark.
But he came at a whistle
and curled tight just above my knees
in the middle of the night.

18.
This is the dawn I want
to fly out of here. I have already
emptied the drawer, folded underwear into my pack.
I stand in the chill,
the half-light, wondering what
foolishness made me leave the familiar.

"Your house is on fire, your children will burn."

All night I slept sitting up.
Through my open window, I saw
trees walking. Black prowlers of the woods
whispered warning, knocked in code on the shingles.
Bats whirred a wind above my head and tiny feet
gained entry, scratched and squealed along the floor.

"Wait. It is not finished yet."

The sun slouches over the yellowing birch grove.
I bend at the woodbox, my breath
beating in puffs. Soon I will sweep the floor,
the mouse droppings left in the dark.

19.
When a forest burns, animals
gather by water. Now the sun
catches leaves in a blossom of fire.
In this setting, I doze
and when the crackling comes, I believe
in a growling and screeching that snag my breath.

At the river, I kneel and cup my hands
to drink. Behind me, the bear
rattles his throat,
rears up, charges. His claws
rake my back and I fall into heat.

Grit of sand and water, flames
snapping, his breath
this weight to bear.
I know the bleeding
only comes from inside, but far away
my daughter cries out with her own dream of it.

20.
Someone's been at my fishing hole.
I find footprints near the river.
Two of them.
A father and son, perhaps?
A husband and wife? Lovers?
When they come together up the path,
I'll be waiting on the porch.

Christ!
Next I'll be stringing barbed wire.

21.
When the sun falls,
oaks pull in their branches
and shadows
creep closer to the cabin.
I am never alone in these woods.

22.
All day. Now night
and the sky still clear. I can see
parts of a constellation through the branches. Perhaps
it is Orion raising his sword
as leaves open tiny doorways for me.

If I were not so afraid
in the dark, tonight
I would walk to the beaver pond.
Never looking over my shoulder, just poking
down the trail, blind woman
with her stick in a world without shadows.
I would come to it on this night.

And the stars: The stars
would gleam first above me,
then reflect in the still water.
I would look down at the bear
and the dog star in Canis
and see that the pond runs deep
as the night sky. And know this.
Tonight. If I had no fear of it.

23.
In the dream, the bear is inside
the house of my childhood.
My mother, a woman poet, my daughter,
all push against a bulging door.
They are trying to keep the bear in the basement,
but I can see his huge, scruffy head, his rubber nose,
his black matted coat through the opening.

In the dream, the bear is chasing me
through all the rooms of my house.
The two of us bounce in great, airy jumps
from bed to bed. He is breaking all the furniture.
When I run to the outer door and yank it open, his woods
sink into a hole. I hesitate,
then slam the door, wait for his paws to take me.

Awake, sweat gathers in my palms,
the moon opens on the ceiling, and my heart
beats as if I had been climbing the ravine.
The *mh, mh, mh, mh* from the bear's throat
still echoes in the cabin. It is only
draft from the stove as embers cool.
When I was a child, I never dreamed
I'd have to hold this beast inside.

24

Once in anger, my mother said
no man would marry me if I kept
my mean disposition.
Now my own daughters scowl and turn
their eyes to men, and my husband
has a heart big enough to hold a month of tantrums.

Still, I come here without them
and turn into this crone, this old woman
who hobbles on her stick along the riverbank,
who mutters deep in her throat
and smells of bear,
who combs her fingers through her hair
and cackles when leaves float down in front of her.

It is almost time. There is no one
who remembers the child, except perhaps
the animals who breathe softly around her.

25.

> Harsh throat of the falls,
> two bends away, half a mile
> from my cabin door.

Groping down the ravine
on a stairway of tree roots,
the roar rising, I sink
into pines, the pitch smell lifting,
the stream rushing down.

> Woman opens to man.
> Mouth, arms, thighs soft as petals.
> She waits for him to enter
> the flower of her.

I climb out on rock,
center of the rapids,
white water boiling, wind
drowning, a thunder
everywhere. Everything
stops breathing.

Long after he leaves, she holds
the wet seed of him, his child
swimming in her darkness.

Boulder below, big as a bear,
crooked pine on the opposite bank,
maple leaf held in the pool.
No shadow, but the fall
of water. All motion caught
blazing in the sun.

When my daughter was born
I wept for three days,
I did not want her
to leave the secret place.

26.
Only light in this cabin is inside
the stove, pine knots
aged how many months, years.
Part of place, like the trout
trapped by falls who fatten and giggle
until they flop off the line, until
the tiny heave of the fisherman's heart dies.

I have captured this wood.
Tonight, its spirit swims in flame.
Dorsal fin, snagged
in the bright river, shivers, glows
until eye dissolves before my eyes.
Can fire bring us alive then?

I rise out of apathy, out of my chair
to the stove, burning
for wet scales, the quiver of gills.
Inside, I know I am
already leaving these woods,
swimming away from shadows
down the highway, another kind of homing.

27.
These trees are past their prime.
Over sixty feet tall, lower branches
stripped of needles, roots
heaved up, bent like arthritic hands.

I fill the front of my shirt
with pine cones. Later, when I rock
on the porch, nodding my head,
I will smell the floor of the woods.

28.
I tried to bury it,
but it's surfaced now.
When the dog slept with me
he was my father.

29.
I am standing in the dump, in back
of the outhouse, with all
the tired things that refuse to decompose.
Plastic jugs, booze bottles, old cans,
the rusted carcass of a stove.

I am digging a grave, three feet by four.
It could hold a child or an animal.
My shovel is long-handled, its blade
nicked and caked with dirt.
It clanks against rocks and my breath
catches when I heave them out.
This is timberland, never meant to be farmed.

In the morning, before I leave these woods,
I will fill this hole and cover it over.
But tonight, sweating from my own effort, my own
animal odor rising, I step away from the hole.
Never looking over my shoulder,
I roll back on these haunches
and let the long, shrill howl rise.
It runs out like a song from my throat.

Yellow Dog Journal

Spring

Welcome, Bear, be thy coming,
Honey-pawed, who now approachest
To our dwelling, freshly-scoured,
To our household, now so charming.
This I wished for all my lifetime,
All my youth I waited for it.
                    —Runo XLVI, *Kalevala*

1.
No clouds for a week. May,
yet this day belongs to summer.
I have bolted my house,
raced north again to woods
that lace the light with new leaves.

Still here. Still here.
Snow holds near the bank,
the Yellow Dog runs full at the bend.
I sing over bumps and puddles,
homing back to the old clearing.

2.
Washout. Road sliced in two
where the swale met a frozen drain,
still water risen from lowland.

Oh glory to feet!
I haul books, food and shirts
the last half mile on my back.

3.
Dusk, the moon waxing
to clarity, trillium and violets
exploding everywhere.

Across the river
a million frogs
fill their throats with song.

4.
I hear it in the river first
and step outside. This rain
has not climbed my hill yet.
Then, tiny pricks
on the roof.

It begins.
Water over water: a perfect time
for love, all the creatures
hiding under leaves.

Alone on the porch, I
whisper familiar names to the wind.

5.
Mice in the woodbox. The fire
still warm, they must think
I am like Gulliver, either dead
or asleep.
They poke their little heads out,
they rattle over newspapers
to eye this intruder
who writes in their giant bed.

Later, in the dark, they will
tie me here
with fine threads from their nests.

6.
Something in the attic.
All night, a ghost
hunts mice above me. I hear
them scurry, then squeal.

It does no good to rise
out of sleep into this cold room.
The hunting comes only
when I sink into dream again.

7.
So cold this morning, my breath
puffs in front of me and my fingers
ache when I hold the pen.
But at least there will be
no rain. Today sun
lights the table top, runs down
to a patch of gold on my sleeping bag,
skims the floor in dusty streaks.

8.
Shooting in the distance:
five shots, then five more.
Breath catches, eyes
jump from the page.

This is Spring, not hunting
season, a time for wildflowers
and mating. I'm sure it is
only boys at target practice.

Still, the doe suspends
her hoof. I will not walk
that hill to the east today.

9.
All winter, my poems
were thin and icy, my head
filled with other people's words.
Those dark months, I lived
in the corners of failure.
Now, here by the river,
the hermit thrush opens his throat,
lines flow over the page, the afternoon sun
warms my shoulders, my back
in its slow circle.

10.
Oh my friend, I wish you
here with me. This evening
I walked upstream where I have never been,
planning to find the source of Bushey Creek.
But the woods were thick and I could see
many bends above me still.
It was not that I was afraid
of losing my way or that night
would come before I found the spring.
It was that there would be no one
to share the mystery, how water

can bubble up out of earth,
then flow into this delicate stream.
So instead, I sat among moss and lichen,
studied the hill on the opposite bank,
then turned back and headed downstream
toward the thunder of the falls.

11.
Violets in a green glass
salt shaker. My face and hands
clean from the river.

I have set a formal table in these woods:
flowers, silverware and wine,
canned beans steaming on my plate.

12.
Beaver lodge begun
below where I dip for water.
Twigs and leaves bending out from the bank,
the river so clear I can see down
to where the log holds below the surface.

I track him up to the beech trees,
the drag mark of his flat tail.

13.
Though nearly midnight,
the sky is dawn's, shadows
of trees balanced against gray.

When I step onto the chill porch
to look for her, the moon
is there. Nearly full,
she forms a cross through the screen: north, south,
east and west, reaching out
to mark us all in lunacy,
to set us mixing days and nights.

14.
Those mice were too bold.
They ran right up to my chair,
across the sink. They peered at me
from around paint cans on the shelf.
Last night I set the traps,
then dreamed I skinned a fox
for the Cherokee woman downstate.
Today I unlock two frozen bodies, look away
from their surprised eyes, try to recall
that woman half-crazed by moonbeams.

15.
Monday, lundi, day
of the full moon, the whole world
working at jobs in villages, cities, on farms.
I have saved the poems of Ryokan for this occasion.
Now, as he speaks to me from his hermitage,
I come to it again: we are all related.

16.
This good French bread
from the Negaunee bakery
has lasted almost a week.

I tear off a piece, then lather it
with butter. I remember
she apologized it wasn't a long loaf.
No doubt, hearing my downstate accent,
she thought I meant to cut it with a knife.
How could she know my tongue
ached to thank her in the northland guttural,
that I would kiss the bread before I ate it.

17.
After dinner, near the beaver lodge,
I watch an osprey follow the flow
downstream, glide, then lift its wings.
It floats the path of clouds.
Upstream, around the next bend, bats
hang in the saplings, waiting for twilight.

18.
This water flows, then catches
in little eddies, almost
trying to run upstream again.
Then it hurries on, tugs
at the bush next to me,
nods the twig at the bend.
It plays the same at the falls,
only louder, with a certain fury.
Here, by my father's sandy beach,
the river is surely a contented woman.

19.
Twenty years ago, with his big Finnish hands,
my father planted these Yellow Dog pines.

Now the tallest is twice his height, and I
am nearly his age when he put them in the ground.
They fan out around the clearing,
green in all seasons, their scent
light in the breeze from the river,
only a few stunted from the hard winter.

20.
Where are the jays this spring?
Now it is the city robin
who is first to call in the morning,
last to sleep at night.

21.
Sometimes I think it is
the waterfall, but I know
it is the wind I hear
long before it arrives
at my clearing. West,
the beech trees are calm
as Ojibwa women in their blankets,
then after the sound of it
they begin to sway in quiet
pleasure. At last it is here,
the smell of rain on the way,
the burning left for another season.

22.
Again, frogs courting.
First one starts, a violinist
trying his bow across the string,
then two or three more tune up.

Then a symphony, along the riverbank,
out of ponds. And the birds,
hidden in a thousand trees.

23.
As darkness settles,
only trillium blossoms
and the bark of birch trees
hold the light.

24.
After ten. Waiting,
waiting on the porch.
First sight, a faint sheen
on the opposite bank. White,
then yellow creeping up.
Then gold.
The wind swirls
now from all directions
as the moon lifts
over the pines, the night
sounds chanting it on.

25.
Oh moon, full again,
oh perfect ball of reflected light,
these crossed haloes,
North, South, East, West,
your brilliance, light
this page I write on, move
me to know this loneliness

of celebration. Who,
there in the other world, is chanting,
praising you? Who hears them,
those she-wolves, howling
and baying as you rise,
as I open my mouth now,
this shadow singing behind me.

26.
Reading the life of Crazy Horse,
then Ryokan's poems. Their
solitude seems natural to me
as I sweep the cabin floor
for the last time this spring.

27
Since I have been here, I have killed
two mice in traps and one bat
I beat to death in the outhouse.
Last night my dreams were colorless.
I think I missed the whir of wings,
the sound of tiny nails on the floor,
fur skimming close to my face. Something
gnaws inside my head. It asks forgiveness.

28
Three ravens screech
and squawk their way
downriver. I remember
when their cry terrified me,

how once they met me
on the road, would barely let me pass,
fluttering their wings,
strutting back and forth.
Now I need no light at night
and walk the trail without a stick,
my feathers nearly formed.

29.

When I last dreamed the bear, he rose
from the earth, the trees
parted in his path, twigs snapping, cracking
from his weight, his flesh
swaying as he lumbered up the hill.

When I last dreamed the bear, he climbed
the stairs to my porch, the rough pads
of his feet brushed in whispers
on the wood: my eyes
sliding back into my head when I turned to face him.

When I last dreamed the bear, he laid
his black head on my thigh,
the bear-smell rising rank around us,
his coat bristling my skin,
the great weight of him leaning, leaning into me.

And though we never spoke,
I knew then that he loved me, and so began
to stroke his rough back, to pull him even closer.

30.
Here, by this pine or that rock,
near these falls, they cupped their palms with river water
like Ripley's father, fisherman turned doctor,
who crooned the words to her.
They dipped their daughters in the stream so that we rose
enchanted, eyes starry in the forest.

No longer theirs, though always theirs
since we fell wet from the mother,
now bound by wing and fur and claw, we come
back and back to their place. Each time
we stand breathless at the edge of light and shadow,
before the river takes us, before we step into its current.

from *Letters to My Daughters*

Your great-grandfather dreamed that his son
would be an engineer, the old man,
the blacksmith with square hands.
To the Finns up north in that snow country
engineer was like doctor today. In the forties
in Detroit, I learned to play the violin.
So did my father when he was a boy in Ishpeming.
He and I never spoke about becoming. Our conversation
was my bow slipping over the strings, my fingers
searching for notes to tell him, his foot tapping time.
That violin cracked ten years ago, it dried out
from loneliness in the coat closet.
Your grandfather, the engineer, sometimes plays his
at night behind a closed kitchen door.
Your grandmother sews and turns up the television.
But what of you two? The piano you practiced over
is still here, a deaf mute in our living room.
I strike an imperfect chord now and remember
we never spoke of dreams.

Once, in Geneva, I saw gypsies. Four of them.
Ravens wearing hats like sombreros.
I stopped still on the sidewalk, was caught by their fire.
I wanted to follow their shadows, drink wine with them.
I wanted to laugh with them, dance with them,
learn all their songs. But your father
touched my arm, told me to speak French
to the policeman, ask directions to our hotel.
Yesterday, Cynthia read a poem about gypsies, how they steal
small children. You were both in Michigan then,
I seldom thought of you on that trip.

She says that her husband laughs, does not believe her
when she whispers how the gypsies came,
flashing their eyes, strolling across the Iowa cornfields.
Listen, you two, if you ever see one in a strange city,
follow him. Think of that fire
he keeps, his house full of urchins.
Those men in Switzerland, they never looked at me.

When I was five or six, I filled my fists
with pansies, velvet yellows and purples
from the neighbor's garden. I meant them for my mother,
somehow to honor the memory of her hands, the smell
of her, those breasts I had aged from.
When I thrust them at her, she frowned and led me back
up the street, my hand still a tight vase.
I cried on Mrs. Bunting's steps, next to her rock garden,
and told her I was sorry. What I meant was
my mother never smelled the flowers or put them into water.
Last spring you, the eldest, brought me
a yellow violet you found while walking home.
Four lemon petals brushed with purple in my palm.
You said, "Look, such a small thing. And perfect."
I lifted it to my face, then on impulse ate it.
We both laughed, but I still taste the tartness.
Now you, the youngest, return with a bouquet of daisies.
They have no scent, I know, but I hold them
to my nose, then pour a pitcher of water,
and never ask you where you picked them.

One gone, the other still here, the two of you
split like Siamese twins must be,
the empty space never to fill completely,
although the other branches out with this pruning.

You, the elder, wanted roots far away
as an ocean. I knew about that
and drove you there, helped you transplant
among men who rhyme. Their language
was a cage to me, but you
were starving for that plotted soil.
"No more wilderness," you cried. "Dead," I said.
No. Not daughter, but mother.
When I left you, I thought of Paris and the guillotine,
of how the accused knows but perhaps never feels
pain until the blade falls. Alone in the car
heading west, I studied against truck lights
my arm, the place where the hand had been.

This week I received two love letters:
one from a boy still in high school, the other
from an older man in his twenties,
a man who whispers about mountains.
Your father doesn't read my mail. He pretends
disinterest in the postmarks, the crimped penmanship,
the shy poems folded inside.
Even when it mattered, he never wrote me. I think he was
embarrassed by misspelled words, stammering lines.
But now he watches me as I watch
for the mailman's truck. He notices
how my fingers stain the curtains when I part them,
that I float through snow in my bathrobe to the mailbox.
I hide the letters in dark drawers and pull them out
when I can't remember my name. They smell like wild violets.
Your father? Lately, I find him bent at his desk,
hands knotted over blank papers. I must tell him
those young men are only in love with poetry.

When I was thirteen, my mother
called the pound to take Patsy away. The dog
was old, a tumor big as a baseball bobbled from her neck.
It was Saturday. I'd been to the movies,
seen Captain Marvel save a whole city.
The truck was pulling away from Northlawn
as I turned the corner. I felt the loss then,
ran home screaming, blaming my mother.
When he was a boy, your father
watched his dog try to jump on a snowbank
out of ruts made by cars. The milkman never saw Fuzzy.
The only witness: a boy who called too late.
Now Softy, with her fur for your faces,
her purrs singing at your ankles,
with her sick bones, has left us.
Real grief drives by sometimes on a sunny day
to corner us. Blame me,
blame anyone if it helps.
This taste of dying is hard to swallow alone.

Even though the plants are only a foot tall,
you, our sixteen-year-old baby, dream them ripe
with fruit, the tomatoes scarlet in their fullness.
And you come flushed from sleep to tell this wealth,
how each night you root through rich soil
to reap the harvest of your first garden.
Nineteen years ago we dreamed your sister,
the child not of our own mating, although we tried,
who came to us, all rosy, at seven weeks
and slept cribbed in the room below ours.
Three times in those first days
we woke at night, eyes blind like moles'
against the lamplight, and groped the sheets,
palms flailing in the empty space between us.

We meant to find her when she cried, to make
her in that space of barren bed
our child, the fruit of love and holding,
before we opened to each other and the space
between us suddenly remembered empty, before we fled
the stairs and soothed the dream
and counted soil for what it was
and took the harvest and felt lucky.

Lunching with you at a restaurant on Commonwealth Ave.
in this alien city of subways and accents,
I smile at your dark hair that wanted to escape the rain
and half-listen to two law students on my left. They are
closer to me than you, cutting your sandwich across the table;
I could touch the arm of the neck-tied young man
next to me, if I wanted. In this crowded place
all conversations blend. "In the case
of Jacobitz vs. Muller . . ." I ask if you need money;
you shake your head and fine wisps lift in the motion.
"Professor Hewitt said we should pay particular attention . . ."
I speak of the woods I just left, but your eyes wander.
She will marry one of these Boston men, I think, as I watch
my neighbor, holding his fork in mid-air, still talking the Bar.
Their hands, I want to tell you. Beware of hands
too pale and soft. These hands have forgotten
the bark of trees. They have never sanded wood to its skin,
never felt rope slide across the palm. These fingers
have never reached into the earth, never touched
the heart of a deer. How can I tell you my fear for children
born of these men, children with vestigial arms,
two fingers to hold a fork, a pen, nothing more.

". . . And when the snows came and everything froze
they slunk close to the back door,
snarling, teeth flashing in moonlight . . ."
It is a father's story of wolves, repeated
nights for his weak, city children
until we grew strong and owned those winters,
blue ice sliding from his eyes to ours
(They did not know what to do, those Finns,
huddled close to the wood stove,
coffee steaming, a draft circling their feet).
". . . And snow drifted around the house,
packed in waves high as the bedroom windows,
and their howls rose from the sea of it . . ."
Listen you two, put your heads
close to mine: blond and dark, then darker.
I want to tell you a mother's story, about sounds
that come in the night, about footprints circling a house.
We never know how to send it away
so we take it in, in here, into this body, this cage.
And when the fire dwindles, when the door flies open,
we rush toward the moon. Fur bristling on our shoulders,
we send shrill cries out through the night.

Even in this bright time for women, you will pass
much of your lives in the kitchen. At last without anger,
that no longer seems wrong to me.
There is pleasure in cooking as well as in eating
and this room, full of good smells and the oven's heat,
sings with the warmth of our making.
Three strong women now, we move our hands
over stove or sink, then turn
from our chopping and stirring to tell what we know.
It is here, heads bent over steaming teacups,
that we read or write letters, here
that we watch for the mail truck.

The tall man who lives in this house knows
how we are and built us a bird feeder. Then he painted it
yellow, and planted it outside our kitchen window.
This morning I sit alone at the table and watch the blizzard
boil into its fifth day. Juncos dart and dip
to the seeds, now a female cardinal shyly drops down.
Her mate, bright in the bare oak, watches over the path,
the long strides your father made through the snow.

This summer holiday your father and grandfather
drift into the yard. Hands in pockets, they rumble
in gutturals about engines or fishing, the words fall away.
Inside, everything mutes. Sunk
into the upholstery, we three
speak politely. Grandmother, mother, daughter: strangers
confused by what was and is. Hemmed between you two,
blood and bone stretch through me, so tight
that when you run a hand over your forehead
in her motion, or lean forward to speak
as she does, I make a pair of fists in my lap
to halt another imitation. This fine, precarious thread!
I remember when she knelt to comb my hair, when, forgive me,
I diapered you. The seamed face
I find in the mirror is the one you know,
not the young woman in my mind's eye.
In this straining, I grow lonely for the girl
locked inside my mother, the one you and I never met,
except in these feathery hands of ours, or how we walk
across the room, or sleep curled to the fabric of our men.

In this house where you bloomed to women, I sift
through the stuff of our rooms, then seal it
in cardboard boxes. Books and dishes. Linens.

The essence of home, now in cartons
halfway to the ceiling. In this leaving, I take
with me pieces of your life as well:
photographs, a misshapen squirrel one of you made
from clay, a vase that held May flowers.
I think we stayed here too long, grew too close to the form
of this place. Now it hurts to break away.
Women are sentimental. It comes from keeping
a house, the daily work we do. Beds and laundry, meals
prepared to be eaten, furniture waxed and rewaxed.
I falter under so many layers
of repetition, even as I gather, discard, possessions.
We do what we have to do. In the precise labelling
I give you this to take with you:
Nothing remains as it was. If you know this, you can
begin again, with pure joy in the uprooting.

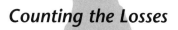

Counting the Losses

Counting the Losses

In her backyard, the flowering crab tree:
first memory, that pink
froth of blossoms. It must have
been May—she was
less than two, not walking yet.
Her parents must have held her
to the flowers. She must have reached for them,
perhaps she said "Mine"
in her one-syllable desire to please.
Her parents must have laughed, the two of them
nearly as innocent as she,
holding up what they had made.
But it was the tree entered her
like blood, food for bone and heart.
"Tree," she would have said, had she
known the word and not just the sense
of bud and leaf, petal, tart little fruit.
This to carry inside: to know branch
and limb. It must have been
her father who carried her, her hands
like blossoms on his shoulders, feeling
roots stretch down to hold on.

Darker, deeper into soil—cutting eyes
out of potatoes, planting them next to
tomatoes, cucumbers, radishes. Raspberry
bushes, webbed and tearing at her cotton blouse,
spiders on the leaves—aphids, potato bugs;
she ate earthworms one day on a dare.

Vegetable garden in the middle of Detroit,
middle of the war, standing in the middle
of the Victory Garden, crab tree in the middle
of it all. Pulling down her underpants
for the neighbor boys in back of the garage,
their weenies peeing gold to the dirt.
Burying Idahos in the vacant lot, roasting them
with Trixie Schultz after someone
chalked swastikas on Trixie's front sidewalk,
right where they played hopscotch and jumprope.
Also, Marcella DeAngelo's visiting aunt
who sat on the porch all of July in her nun's habit
shrieking that children should be quiet.

Learning to take in this darkness, feeling
it churn and pile up like pieces of coal the coalman
poured down the chute, his face grimed, hands
smearing his overalls, his truck, whatever he touched.
Beginning to love this darkness so that
when she stood in the light and tried to walk
Ruthie Rich's back fence after sniffing an old
ammonia bottle from the alley, she fainted and fell off,
wind knocked out of her, and she thought
she might be dead. Finding the washerwoman
in Ruthie's dark basement who must have
been blinded from the sun and fallen down the stairs,
seeing blood on her face, seeing the broken eyeglasses,
the stretcher when the ambulance came, learning a silence
of breath held. And Ruthie's own father
who worked in produce at the A&P—and still there wasn't
food enough for company in that house of eight kids—
him telling about tarantulas that scurried
from the green banana bunches, huge and hairy-legged,
bigger even than the cockroaches in Detroit's sewers.
"They bite," he said. "They'd kill you dead."

❧

Learning to fear the darkness, yet wanting to know
everything that entered her small world in that big city.
Kneeling on the couch in her living room, hanging
over its back, peering through the curtains to spy
on Rosie the Riveter kissing each man who brought her
home from the night shift in his Chevy or Ford.
Making a game out of counting gold stars
hung on sleazy rayon banners
framed in gold fringe in neighborhood windows.
Studying comic books so she'd be able to tell
Japs from Chinamen, something about
the slant of eye and space between the toes—she
couldn't understand it yet.

Couldn't understand the roiling and pitching
inside her, the "I wants" crowding up and out
of her mouth. When she got the red
two-wheeler finally, she took it around the block
by herself, zigging and wiggling over the sidewalk.
It was August, her eighth birthday, and she spilled
as soon as she got around the corner
out of her parents' sight. Skinned knees and a dent
in the rear fender, joy of the gift suddenly spoiled,
shame as she walked it back, metal scraping the tire.

Shame when she had to return the flowers
she'd picked from Mrs. Bunting's rock garden.
Shame when her two-year-old brother pointed at the black man
in the shoe store and asked why his face was dirty.
Shame at her father's accent.
Shame at her mother's housedress
and anklets under wedgies. Shame
when the boarder next door held her on his lap
and touched where he shouldn't have.

✣

How to let it go.
How to keep on—
not like the freshly-sheared sheep
hiding in a corner of the pen,
whose coat always grows back to be
sheared again for blanket, sweater,
wool scarf for someone's daughter.

Letting go of place: Kick the Can in the alley,
scrub baseball in the street.
Exchange it for oak and birch, a lake
that would swallow her,
fury of storms, sirens calling.
Letting it fall away: the house
on Northlawn torn down for an expressway.
Now pheasant on the fence, deer in the fairway,
snow drifted to the window sill.
Letting the rift mend: no more
sidewalk and streetlight, no museum, no Ballet Russe,
just open field, red-winged blackbirds
calling, rush of wind through the pines.
Letting the child go: Ghost of the past
covered by its own darkness—cloak, shroud,
black skin of the bear.
She'd never meant this to happen,
never meant to put on a wanderer's shoes.

Haines saying, "I mean . . . the work, and the life, must have their
origin in a place of conviction for the poet."

Which is, in part, why Akhmatova cried out during the purge,
even after she'd had to burn her poems: "I am not one of those
who left the land."

Dear Becky followed her husband from Michigan to Connecticut: "When I went away from all things, when I left the place / (my feet knew, . . . I wanted to cry. . . ."

For "there is . . . a genius of place, a presence, and because there is, people's feelings accumulate about it" from Wright.

"We *are* it / it sings through us," says Snyder.

Lawrence called it a spirit: "We cannot see that invisible winds carry us, as they carry swarms of locusts, that invisible magnetism brings us as it brings the migrating birds."

Atwood in Canada: "How else can you live but with the knowledge / of old lives continuing in fading / sepia blood under your feet?"

And Hugo at White Center: "When you say, 'I live here,' animals / you hadn't thought of for years live on your lawn. / They insist you remember their names."

Wright again. He always knew: "In this field, / Where the small animals ran from a brush fire, / It is a voice / In burned weeds, saying / I love you."

    O Spring.
Wanting to stop the car on the Leelanau Peninsula
and walk through the cherry orchard, wanting to walk
on white petals, white under her feet, white falling on her hair.
The band of bluebirds that fed on her lawn
for three days, blue in the light, blue against the new grass,
before they flew to their nesting place.
    O Bone.
White trillium turning to pink, pushing through moist April loam
in the woods up the hill from her meadow house.

Don't forget the ocean, blue as the blue tiles on the roof
of that beach house in Florida, the same blue
pelicans sculpted on each corner of the eaves.
Mating dance of snowy egrets in the salt marsh
in Arcata, California, snow on the mountains behind them.
Blue iris in the vase inside her rented house, their beautiful
fan like slow wings spreading. Her own arms opening
to jewels of hummingbirds at the feeder—darting, suspended,
then buzzing and clicking—red throats, green
wings—gold, real gold, for crowns.
     O Heart.
Erotic lichee nuts in the mouth. Scent of sex
on the sheets, night jasmine through the open window.

Aristotle said it: "The female is as it were a deformed male . . ."

Confucius too: "One hundred women are not worth a single
testicle."

"Blessed art thou, O Lord our God and King of the Universe, that
thou didst not create me a woman" still used as a daily prayer by
the Orthodox Jewish male.

"Every woman should be overwhelmed with shame at the thought
that she is a woman" taught by St. Clement of Alexandria.

Freud telling the world that women were "castrated men," thus
they suffered from "penis envy."

Milton called her "a fair defect / of Nature."

And that 19th century physician: "It is almost a pity a woman has
a womb."

> Witch, hag, crone, harpy, shrew, old maid, wallflower, whore,
> trollop, chippie, temptress, bitch, pig, dog, doll, baby, old lady,
> momma, Medusa. Angel.

"I don't look at myself as a commodity, but I'm sure a lot of people have," Marilyn said in a *Life* interview shortly before she died.

Tennyson in "The Princess": "Man for the field and woman for the hearth . . . / man to command, and woman to obey."

Hawthorne detested the "damned mob of scribbling women" and their "trash."

And Longfellow, sneering: "What we admire in woman, / Is her affection, not her intellect."

Mailer, of course: "(Women) weren't born to be free, they were born to have babies."

"If I wish to define myself, I must first of all say: 'I am a woman'; . . . a man never begins by presenting himself as an individual of a certain sex," said de Beauvoir.

Finally, Levertov in the 60s, long before Chicago's "Dinner Party": "and if . . . a white sweating bull of a poet told us / our cunts are ugly—why didn't we / admit we have thought so too?"

> *Cunt, clit, slit, trench, twat, sewer, hole, pit, flap, trap, snatch, beaver, chicken lips, split-tail, bearded clam, douch-bag. Vagina Dentata.*

How to be a woman in this universe, no steps to follow.
She can't be her mother. Both her grandmothers
in the ground—and not them either,
nor her California aunt, married three times and
dead on the operating table in '77. Not her great-aunt,
whose memory held until her 93rd year though she was
sentenced to that nursing home by her only daughter.

Not even the three Finnish aunts in Ishpeming,
receding together in the house of their childhood.
But they gave her part of it: "We survived because we
had to." She saw their backs straighten, their hands
steady in their laps. She thought of snow
blowing around their house, no wood for the stove,
and wolves at the door, the forest dark and close.
And she walked the bridge they made.

Not Wollstonecraft, not Woolf, not Emily locked in.
How to be a woman for her daughters,
her son, when she couldn't live
like their friends' mothers, though she spent
a fourth of her life with hobbies and shopping and PTA,
the schism a gaping mouth in her dreams.
How to be a woman to her man,
not wanting to serve like her mother, not able
to stay in her place in his place. The crabapple tree
gone, nothing of hers to replace it.
How to hold the heart together when it wants to fly off
in so many directions, when her people move west and east,
their lives boxed up in cartons, only knowing
"we all would have died for our children."
Not Adrienne, not Stein, not Sarton on the other coast.

How to love women without being "in love" with them.
How to love men without losing her self.
How to stand naked as a woman in the eyes of women
just becoming women. How to be sure.
Talking with women, the trust growing,
seeing light around the bodies of Tillie, Deena,
Diane, Maxine, Teresa, Anne Marie, her dead cousin Babe.

Not Plath in her oven nor Sexton wrapped in her mother's fur coat.
"Nothing we have said will go any further,"
they swear to each other as women do,
but her words came back to her in three days.

Learning to forgive women, learning to accept
her own weaknesses and those of her sisters, though
her true sister was a blue baby and she can't forget
her guilt at living while her mother mourned.
"Eat of the fruit." And Eve did.
She does, has, and will again, she knows,
temptation surfacing, snakes in both her hands.

Impossible to hold on, the anger
like wind slipping through her fingers.
Learning to question
George Washington, Pope John, Doctor Spock,
Professor, Lawyer, Banker,
every Man she has ever known.
    "No"
churning in her head, her dreams.
Learning to say
    "I"
    "Me"
    "Us"
meaning "Woman."

And yet, our fathers were our first loves.
We miss their hands and voices, their step in the house,
the scent of pipe and shaving lotion, sweat and whiskey breath.

Diane lost hers early, that sailor
who came and went, loving adventure not her mother
who slept on one side of the bed, the other side
waiting, unwrinkled and empty. How can
a daughter take her mother's place, how can a daughter
save a bed for her father?

When Linda's died in Springfield, Illinois,
it was Spring. It was cancer and he was
in his own bed, his own living room.
They'd been waiting all winter: her sister,
her brothers, her mother, over coffee at the kitchen table.
His daughter put her hands on his temples,
his wife laid hers over his heart, his two carpenter sons
held his carpenter hands. Hands holding on,
hands over hands, hands with him while he finished what he had to.

Susann's, also from cancer. She heard the siren
a mile away and dropped her tennis racket and ran.
Again, Mary's from cancer. Tall and straight, he made
all that money to show his father-in-law he could.
Alice's left by the gun. That morning the neighbors
trampled the pachysandra, peering in through the living room window.
When Lillian's went, she was with him—old man
who never let his women enjoy. "Stop that giggling," he'd rumble,
so quiet she never saw his rage. "You've had enough fun."
She carried that on to her marriage, never knew
till too late that laughter was allowed in bed.

It was Teresa at the bookstore who taught her.
"My father died this year," she said. "My daughter is only four."
Teresa hadn't known about being a mother or giving birth,
never knew about dying, had to learn from her daughter:
What does Heaven look like? How will Grandpa get there?
What will he do when they let him in? Who else is there?
If he's watching over us, why can't he call us up?
I think he's here inside you, Mama, just like I was.

"Death? Why this fuss about death. Use your imagination, try to
visualize a world *without* death" from Charlotte Perkins Gilman
(1860-1935), the American writer.

Simone Weil (1910–1943) on another continent: "Death and labour are things of necessity and not of choice."

Eleanor Roosevelt (1884–1962), nine years after FDR died: "Life has got to be lived. That's all there is to it."

And Margaret Mitchell (1900–1949), writing one novel all her life from her sickbed: "Life's under no obligation to give us what we expect. We take what we get and are thankful it's no worse than it is."

Kathe Kollwitz (1867–1945), whose life was her art: "I am afraid of dying—but being dead, oh yes, that to me is often an appealing prospect."

George Eliot (1819–1880), in a letter to Sara Hennell: "The years seem to rush by now, and I think of death as a fast-approaching end of a journey—double and treble reason for loving as well as working while it is day."

"I contemplate death as though I were continuing after its arrival" from Pearl Buck (1892–1973), the childless mother of hundreds of children.

And anthropologist, Ruth Benedict (1887–1948), speaking of strong women: "They have made of their lives a great adventure."

Florida Scott-Maxwell (b. 1883), who began her journal in her 82nd year: "You need only claim the events of your life to make yourself yours."

And Nadine Stair, 85 years old, from Louisville, Kentucky: "If I had it to do again, I would travel lighter than I have. . . I would start barefoot earlier in the Spring. . . I would go to more dances. . . ride more merry-go-rounds. . . . I would pick more daisies."

✣

This journey takes years, goes fathoms
deep, and there's no turning back.
Let the dead hawk go
and the family of orioles scattered by the road.
Let the squirrel go,
innards singing from his mouth.
Let the sheep go,
white skin empty in the pasture.
Let your grandmother go.
Let her shadow stop swaying on the wall.
Let the rope go. Let the knife go that cut her down.

Say "Tree." Say it, say "Tree." Tree. Isn't that what
that wall-eyed poet told her years ago? "Go back to tree,"
he'd said, "every tree you've ever known."

Begin with crabapple. Begin with Spring,
begin with blossoms, begin with Father:
White birch near the Yellow Dog, her father
wanting to show her each secret place that was his.
Smooth skin, white gleaming in dark woods.
"I love these trees," he'd said, and wrapped his arms around one.
Something lifted from the ground, something white, and flew.
He knew it was his last trip to the river.

Birch: Once, cross-country skiing,
she'd come upon a stand, all white along the Big Betsy.
Snow fell, white sinking into snow, black veins
burned on the bark like a negative.

Pine: Tallest ones she'd ever seen, two
joined by Ojibwas maybe, grown around a rock into a seat
for two, for lovers maybe. He'd put two stones there,
where they'd sat, when they left to go back to town.

Redwood: Rough, spongy bark—seven sisters
growing in a ring around the burned one.
She'd crawled into its cave, what was left of it,
and watched the sky float by above her.

Cedar, Cypress, Eucalyptus.
Blue Spruce, Oak, Willow.
Maple, Basswood,
Ginkgo, Chestnut.

This is what goes on, bearing
branch and limb. Leaf, needle.
Scent of blossom. Gift of fruit and seed.
This to carry inside. Tree. This word
flowing through. This small word to survive.

from *Dancing the Fault*

Missing me one place search another,
I stop somewhere waiting for you.
—*Walt Whitman*

Meeting My Father at the River

On this evening path from camp
to river's bend, shadows
roll over and lie down in hollows,
then rise from rotting stumps
to drift along the lowland.
They stalk my boots' dull thud, branches
opening, closing overhead.
The cabin's lamp, the glowing stove
burn behind me now in memory.

At the river, my father
still stands in light.
This will be his last trip to these waters.
His arm lifts, his line wavers,
settles over the pool.
I have often dreamed this motion:
me watching from the bank, him casting,
the whir of reel, the bend and dip of rod and arm.
Now a small trout rises to the fly.

He calls, "I got one!"
It surfaces, flickering in wetness.
He is pleased I am here to witness
and leans with grace in hip boots
for the ritual of netting,
stepping sure as a young man again.
"Good one," I cry, and wave.
He wades slowly out of sight
around the bend, creel bumping at his side.

From the Underworld

"Bats tangle in your hair," she apologizes,
hands stammering. A shiver
of wings darkens the room.

He chased it with a broom. She cowered
in their bed, head buried.
A faint sound: I don't know
if it was a woman's voice calling.

Preposterous vision: Her arm casting
over the stream, the rod
quivering, no fly. Plastic
rainbonnet tied under her chin, her dark
curls beneath the transparency.

The boat becalmed, tethered to land at Fayette.
We hiked through the ghost town
to woods, heard inchworms chewing oak leaves.

At dusk we drank coffee on the stern. They began
to fall like leaves in a wind. We thought they were
kingfishers at first, darting for mayflies.

They hang in the saplings
waiting for twilight.
The riverbank is full
of the harvest, these
pendants with wings.

Our fear nearly smothers us.
I know a woman
from Guam whose lashes rest long
on her cheekbones, who dreams them
through the heat of summer nights.

❀

Once, late, in a parking lot,
I heard a soft *ki, ki.*
Above the streetlight
I caught the sense of them, floating.

❀

Someone spied it, cringing on top of the kitchen cupboard.
James came with a dishtowel,
made a knapsack and carried it to daylight.

He said it was a mouse-angel.
The women twittered like sparrows.

❀

Sitting in the outhouse,
I felt a whisper near the patched shingle, saw
the tiny face by my shoulder, miniature hands
pulling the body through the knothole,
delicate ears, soft gray fur.

I picked up a board and beat
against the wall in a frenzy,
that space already filled with his presence.

❀

I am often lonely at night.
Sometimes I think of you, your arms
folding me close,
the life we might have had.

Ironing

The pattern flows. Leaves and flowers blend, a river spinning over the cotton. It is my daughter's blouse. Green ripples under my fingers. Pink and blue blossom under the iron's steam. Tiny buds. The cement floor presses its back against the soles of my feet. The pipes gather pearls of moisture. I am a tree. I rise from the earth. I shade the ironing board. My hand passes back and forth, a branch in the wind. One sleeve, then the other.

Summer, but this basement remembers winter and holds loam to its heart. The water in these pipes wants to go underground, back to the dark. It is June, and my daughter sleeps in the heat of her dream. She is far from my belly now, on her white bed, still as a breath in the hospital wing. I have washed the blood from her blouse. Now the iron passes over a sleeve, it curls around a button. Colors intertwine, tangle. The petals blur. They bleed into leaves on the vines.

The car was thick with glass, little beads of glass, blue and yellow in the sun. The lace of slivers of glass, glistening on her skirt, under her bare feet. Glass clinging to her blouse, her skin. Glass in the upholstery, on the carpet, the dashboard. Prisms in the sun. A clink and tinkle like wind chimes when she stirred. Her hands gliding to her face. Glass glinting in her hair. Blood shining on the glass. Glass flowing, separating, as she stirred on the seat of the car.

I pass the iron over her blouse. Steam hisses. I hear her voice as she is lifted from the car. Steam rises from the flowers, the petals. The leaves. I am a tree. Her long hair matted with blood, the cut open on her scalp. My feet curl like roots on the floor. Sweat gathers on the pipes. I rustle over her blouse. Her hair unfurls on the pillow. The flowers blend, the leaves blur. My hand glides over the pattern, a river spinning. Her dream flows without sound. Steam hisses from the iron. Petals and leaves mingle pink and blue. Green. I am ironing her blouse. Only this motion is left.

Trying to Remember

—for Deena

A note from my friend on this morning of the first snowfall. Slow waxing in letters exchanged, tones and contours spelled into words. Each envelope holds a mirror of feeling: two women naked in each other's eyes.

A month ago, close talk with this man I love, over cheese and wine at the kitchen table. Drifting to food after languorous hours of hands fluttering, spiralling cries. We are lonely already. We want to fly back to the body.

She carries the dark side of the moon under her shawl. I catch sun in a crystal by my window. We approach middle age together. Our words spin over trees, trill in strands, a sparrow's song. Between us, we create another woman.

Our fingers meet on the knife handle. Embarrassment at the collision, hands leaping away. We try to come together with words, but his coyote eyes glitter, a wolf rises up through my bones.

She writes what her grandmother said: If you wash your face in the first snow, you will have a beautiful complexion. Letters or books, something to hold in the hand. Her words are always a gift.

This good bread. We tear off chunks to eat with our cheese. He swirls wine in his mouth before swallowing it. Grandmother said we must honor bread, he tells me. You must kiss it before you eat it.

Summer afternoon, my grandmother. Perhaps I am four or five. I am sitting on her lap. She is humming, I think. It is hot and we have nothing to do, no chores, no one to play with. We want and we do not want something.

Walking in the woods, first snow sifting through pines, white puffs of breath, leaves under my feet slightly muffled. The ground disappears, a veil shudders over the land.

She speaks of fire burning as her sons grow past her. I say my childhood ran away when I turned my back for a moment. She is pleased with this transformation. We change, she writes.

Ferns along the path are still green, though they are growing white skins. The weight of the snow bows the stems to the ground. It is cold and the fronds do not move when I pass.

When I sat on her lap, her fingers spun over my arm, her fingers traced lacy patterns on my skin. We were both half-asleep. She was humming, I think. The breath of her love on my arm.

The ferns, bent from such a little snow. A fallen birch across the path.

His hands burn, set me trembling. The moon whispers and sighs with our caring.

I was so close to her heart then, her fingers pulsing over my arm.

Snow touches my cheeks, my eyelids. The birch lies on top of the snow.

We are waking, she says. We have only been hibernating.

We must honor it. His hand holds the bread to his lips.

Snow keeps falling. My tracks must be covered by now.

I am trying to remember what my grandmother told me.

Orchids

1.
Service for townsman, old sailor
whose face I barely recall, except
as it raised
to catch telltales on the jib.

I rise with incense and candle flame
to alleluias rolling in waves.
A long time, Father,
since I faced
linen touched to chalice, the breaking of wafer.
I can't help
the hand-stitch at my breast, this genuflection.

2.
We float like dreams in our funeral clothes, third car
behind the hearse, this time the uncle
who was mean and crotchety,
surgeon whose fingers finally
twisted so crooked he couldn't hold his cigar,
who never shut off the television
and let conversation fall to his wife.

Past elms, old houses
turned into offices, past storefronts blinking OPEN,
past the Black man on Peck Street,
hat over chest, standing
with head bowed until we all roll past.

3.
Up North near Cross Village
in the divided cemetery, I step over
a wire fence
to low graves and bend to Ojibwa names.
This is the paupers' side.

When the earth goes soft, falls
under my feet,
I think I will sink down to them,
except for the crow that shrieks,
beating wings under my ribs.

4.
They roll the drawer shut on her
and I hear a woman
crying. The voice is glass shattering
on the mausoleum floor.

My chair scrapes. I stand
like stone for this suicide. My daughter
unfurls inside my belly
to take hold of her aunt's name.

5.
My own aunt saw her dead mother once
in a moth
battering its wings against the kitchen door.

Last year, when her heart stopped in California, she found me
sleeping in a hotel room in Michigan.
In the dream, we held hands. Her pulse
trembled against my thumb.

6.
There is no end to this, reader.
My friend was a warrior, yet even she quit.

I sat with her before she left,
but we couldn't make the journey together. Her breath
was fragile as an orchid's petal.
She was already floating in air.

Celebrating the Mass

In this hospital room, lacking the hands
of a nurse, I braid my daughter's hair
into corn rows. She is nineteen now.
When did I stop touching my child?
We have eaten sandwiches brought in and picked
at food on her tray, then turned to the mirror.
Helpless in these weeks of testing, waiting,
we want to alter her life in some way.

I think of those other mothers who have done this,
their backs aching, their hands tightening.
I think of them standing long hours
on porches of farm shacks maybe, or in tenement rooms.
I think of them weaving dark strands
to make their daughters beautiful
after the meals were served, after
the mending, the washing hung, the fields hoed.

Here, a comb sets our boundaries.
Fingers separate and part, we begin
another row: blond hair lifted, pulled,
the pattern worked in. I sculpt to the shape of bone.
Now six braids done. Now an hour. Now nineteen years.
We learn each other again. Hands to head,
fingers knitting a cap, we begin
at the temple, around the ear, crown to nape.

Purple Finches

They come in the morning. Even before she is awake, she hears the tap-tap of their beaks, a scratching, faint whistles in the air. When sun drifts along the bed, she floats to the surface.

They ripple over the feeder. The males flame in the light, their pink and rose feathers. The females are delicate, softer. She wants to say, "Look, they are beautiful," but there is no one. They fly up and wait in the pines, then sink back.

The window mutes their voices. She circles the room slowly so they won't startle. They bend to the seeds and crack them with their beaks. They were not here yesterday or the day before. They will not come tomorrow. She puts her finger to the glass and enters their rhythm. She steps inside their color.

The Cottage Poems: Lake Michigan

1. Entering
I have taken this cottage out of season.
Now it is just these two old women and me
who finish summer without ornament.
From my window, I watch
them squirrel along the path,
their arms full of blankets and sheets. They will
board up another cabin today.

Once, everything was new here: rusted lawn chair,
broken grill, iron rail leaning out from its post.
(Perhaps that hunchback held dark men in her arms.
Did her sister swim under the moon?)
Even inside, paint curls from the window sill.

Behind me, the refrigerator wheezes,
the screen door bangs shut. Sand
blossoms from my feet
running down the dune to the beach.

2. The Storm
All afternoon, wrestling with words at the desk, heat
kneading the moist air. My pinned-up hair
wants to escape and my throat closes,
remembering deserts, trying to remember
how to sing. Today
even the flies are fierce as sharks,
swimming around my legs.

We are waiting for something to happen.

It begins first near the sink, a gasp of air drawn in:
pressure sinking, then rising.
When the trees shake their fists at the lake,
I cross my arms and watch from the doorway.
A flash low at the horizon, then the wind
surges in waves—a breath
on my skin, the hand passing over my forehead.

3. Monarchs
Each year they sail back, falling before the leaves.
They dip and flutter, the air full
with orange petals, to kiss the warty pods.

Outside my door, this dune field
of milkweed and goldenrod;
bright, hairy drupes dragging down the sumac;
acorns hailing on the roof.

So many butterflies scattered on the beach.
Wings broken, they tremble against shore
like children tearing away.

4. Waves
Yesterday, the lake
slept without breath, hands
still as a woman waiting.
Morning, the clouds slid over her.
Evening, the sun ran away.

Today she stirs, shakes
white froths of hair.
I feel the mood of this stretching,
this swinging of arms.

If I could, I would descend
the fragile stairs with a sail,
leap naked into the waves,
lift out over the blue skin—
I am that restless.

5. Inside
All this rain:
The cottage stands limp
under dripping eaves.
    Everything—
    curtain, rug, blanket, cushion
    —swells
with the weight of water.
Even the eyelids
heavy, and the mind
swims in the pool of it.
I pass this day
wading
from window to drizzly window.

6. Healing
Half a week spent drowning in rain.
Below, the lake calls
in its dim voice, and fog
hangs on the dune. Everything
clings, like this sand to my boots.

    Enough.

All the way out to the road
stretch woods, a cave of oak and pine.

Another who suffered from rain
carved a path through them once.

    Deeper,

to the center of rotting timber.
—Oh chanterelle, amanita, agaricus,
glowing fruit of rain. Oh parasols,
oh hedgehogs, earthstars. Oh fairy ring,
you must be what I was looking for.

7. The Cardinal

It was the cardinal, the bright male,
who brought me out on the dune
that last evening. He was chipping
from a dead branch near the sumac,
the wind catching his tail feathers,
bending them southward so that he looked
broken but oddly comical on his perch.

There was no time to lift the glasses.
It took only four wingbeats
to clear the sumac, then the blowout,
and pass over the pines to the north.
White head and tail,
bald eagle hunting the shoreline home,
just the red bird and me standing witness.

9/22
Still this.
As I climb the apartment stairs,
I worry that the phone will ring,
stop ringing,
before I turn my key in the lock.

10/7
This morning rain drifts
to another town. Now the whole courtyard
sleeps, its moist mouth silent.
    No. A blackbird
    calls.
    Another answers
    (water beading on red shoulders).
    Now a sparrow
    cleanly fills the air and the pheasant
    echoes from pools in the cornfield.
We are all surfacing from dream,
shaking our heads,
as drops fall from the eaves
in no particular pattern.

11/15
At last, a bird at the suet cake.
Welcome goldfinch, king of my balcony,
strutting this railing,
sunflower seed in your beak.

1/16
Third day of the blizzard.
Locked up in these rooms, pacing
and calling for friends,
I end at the window again.

Once, somewhere, was land,
the before of this white sea below.
I stand watch
over an ocean of snow, over waves

that swirl or rise in peaks.
I am a stone
sinking and this building
a ship that shudders, sways,
then lumbers but makes no headway.

1/22
Sun lights a million fires
over snow, tiny crystals of water.
This bright morning blurs
all memory of storms and the heart
soars in a celebration of blue.

Skis clamped to my boots, I push out,
a heron, across the meadow.
I am light,
a feather on the surface. I cross
the field, glide and stroke. Glide again.

In this whispering, I try to remember
wings. My tracks
show where I came from, courtyard
small as a bird's eye.
Ahead still, the dark woods.

3/7
Thaw long in coming. With a roar
the roof shakes off its burden,
and in the meadow, briars
poke through the crusty snow.
This holy Tuesday
the big oak across the field
blossoms with blackbirds, singing.

3/25
When I found him in the furrow,
only a foot and wing left,
I brought him home to a bed of pine cones.
　　Tonight his foot
　　claws and flexes on the cave wall
　　of this apartment, and his epaulet
　　shines gold in the candlelight.
We see what we want to see.
I live here suspended, knowing a blackbird
takes flight now over pine trees.

Six Poems for Nine Crows

After a painting by S. Krause in Philip Booth's apartment.
—Syracuse, New York

September now.
Only a breath of summer remains.
Uprooted, I stand at this eastern window
and watch sparrows drift from the maple
like brown leaves. I own nothing here,
the eye clear in new air.

Owl feather, finch petal, jay leaf,
flicker branch, pheasant stem:
feathers dropped in passage. Now I
plant them near his painting of crows in a field.
            One flaps his wings
            at a newcomer, beak open
            and shrilly warning. Another
            stands guard. The rest
            tend to the harvest.
These silent relics bloom
in their vases, each vein
of color defined, barbs
still poised to the flight.

Wherever we live, those we care about
find us, and we wait for their letters.
They glide from post office to mail box like homing pigeons,
the heart inside pulsing "Friend."

Now this news about rifles and chain saws
ripping Mohawk trees, about SWAT teams,
about women hiding in their houses, this plea to help
a stubborn elder who tried to save the trees

makes my hands heavy.
600 miles west of here, and north,
are other woods. I'm a fool to imagine
no one has timbered that land since I left it.

"Philip's tree."
There, I've named it, the maple
outside my bedroom window. I know it
belongs to itself and I'm only a renter here
—still, he's told me the pleasure it's given,
so these words are for him.

In this gale wind, far from the sea, your tree
flaps its wings and turns wild.
It means to lift up, soar back to its mother, back
to the shade, the dark seed of before.
I witness it all from your window.
The wind calls through a thin crack,
even this paper flutters.

The station begun, though I'd meant to wait
a month for the earth's shell to form.
First a gossipy jay, then a grackle in mourning.
Now today, a convention of sparrows.
The whole balcony flickers brown. They feed
like horses at the trough, queue up on the railing for turns.
The thinkers take the floor and spilled seed,
beaks opening, closing, to the glory of food.

Last week, driving in the country, the sun barely risen,
I passed a farmer in overalls, bucket heavy at his side.
(He is crossing to his sheep. They nearly dance
at his coming, black faces nudging each other by the fence.)
We all tremble for something—the hand
to reach into the slop pail, a letter,

This place belongs to others. Stretching out
in these rooms, I sense the skin of their lives.
Walls don't keep secrets.
Each breath that seeps from our lungs
leaves a thread clinging to plaster or fabric,
a chorus of whispers humming.
The monstrous shadow rises and falls without the body,
and we long for them to join again.
In this half-light, dark wings
burst open, the maple scratches at the window.

Letter About the End of All Flesh from California to the Snow Country

Oh Friend, how apart we are. Here it rains,
seven days and seven nights. Do you remember
this torrent, now in your white silence
(puff of breath, crunch and creak of boot on snow)?
Do you recall the fury
of water rising, water falling, the surge
and rush, the flow, this awful thrust?

It rains. Nothing here is white.
The ocean casts up timber in its foam
as if to toss the tree roots back to land again.
It beats at wharf and bridge
and shore. The earth gives up.
It breaks away, slides down the hills,
drags house and pine and roadway in its oozing trail.

How could you feel this in your cold
and quiet time, this rain that falls through night and day?
From the cliff, I watch
whales spouting, on their mating trip to Baja.
In the canyon, all this damp and soggy week,
an echo of someone pounding nails,
building that ship to follow them.

—Santa Cruz, California

127

Letter About Guilt from California to the Snow Country

Last week, rain fell in a rage,
dragging its muddy hair over the hills.
Flood waters rose, walls and roofs caved in,
redwoods slid and buried lovers in their beds.
Now this warm Monday, sun
spreads out in the pasture and I've peeled back
my clothes to the skin. A coyote
straggles from the manzanita grove and monarchs
dry their wings over the poppies.

Friend, halfway across the country, you suffer
a different climate. Where you are, firemen
wear coats of ice and water freezes
when it hits the burning building. On Lake Michigan
waves break in crystals against the churning boat.
—But I'm trying to speak of guilt, how I
stayed dry, how I'm stealing warmth
from this winter. I'm thinking about that cardinal
singing in your snow-covered pine tree.

                              —Santa Cruz, California

The Gray Whale

Before the advent of motorized sailing vessels, it is believed that
certain species of whales could communicate across hemispheres.

1. Inside the Whale's Head—Santa Cruz, California
We climb to get there, to what seems
only rock or rubble from a distance.
My friends want to play,
but I'm new to the coast, still afraid
of what comes with the waves, undulating—
the long strands of kelp, sea palms
and weeds, whatever curls in on itself.

> It must have known it could not go back
> to fluid motion and grace, even as it
> rose from the deep, gave its bulk to the tide.
> I was inland when it beached. I didn't witness
> the passage of breath, the souvenir hunters,
> the mourners. My friends saw
> the helicopter lifting it in pieces.

No one warned me about this.
Above the sea now, it bakes in the sun
—flesh gone to the air, the rest
growing into the earth. We walk
the length of the spine in our small shoes,
we touch the stumps of its bones, we circle
the jaw, we give away our words.

> I am nothing when I stand inside its head.

2. The Fisherman Calling—Davenport Landing, California

The fisherman stands far out on the rocks.
He is past the cove and we're just two women
who haven't learned the ocean. We watch him
cast and cast again through our binoculars
—his rod glints, the rocks glisten,
waves fall and fall on each other.
This once was a whaling station. We came looking
for spouts, but find only a man fishing morning away.

When he waves his arms, we think he has fallen or is
trapped by the tide. The speck of him grows in the lens.
He waves, and we follow a path along the spine of the cliff
past alyssum and poppy, foam and crash of surf.
The wind whips our hair, our feet rattle stones
—past thorn and stubble of grass—the sea
booms against the rocks as we go to save the fisherman.

When we stand above him, we still don't see.
He cups his hands and shouts, but the wind
takes his voice. Then he points to the water
below us. It rises, gray
mottled skin. It heaves its weight up.
Side and fluke. Eye. It dives and explodes again
—the sea churning, the wind blowing,
the four of us joined each time in the air.

3. Following By Boat—Eureka, California

Gale winds for a week. Now a drizzle
settles the sea, and our rented boat
throbs over the bar, out of the harbor.
Binoculars and cameras hanging from our necks,
we pretend to be experts, not eager
for bubbles, for spouts, for seabirds flying low.

They are here, they are waiting.
They listen to our chatter, our jokes and our laughter.
Their shadows drift under the hull.

Now they rise to port, to port.
Five giants.
Five monsters spangled with barnacles.

Now dancers leaping in unison
—buffalo, tiger, whatever has left us—
hill and rock, curve and sway of the universe.

From the mouth of Mad River, they touch,
to the mouth of the Eel,
past Table Bluff—they touch, they touch.
Loop and slide of the dream, rolling over and under.
Body and drum—beside us, in front.
They touch. They sigh. They touch.

All this we've lost.
All this—forgotten.

Hawk

Dead hawk outside my bedroom window,
even the cats won't touch it.
I laid low for three days,
didn't leave the house,
and wrote my Cherokee friend.
He hasn't answered, the hawk's
been waiting. Today I took

the tail feathers and feet.
I feel worst about the feet,
hanging from the backporch beam—
fists clenched, claws like my own hand
holding the knife. I knew
when the other one flew over, keening,
he wouldn't recognize her like that.

—Jacoby Creek, California

132

A Sense of Place

There is a genius of place, a presence, and because there is,
people's feelings accumulate about it.

          —James Wright

I

I recall that California yard full of caged birds
we used to drive past on the way to the ocean
and the parrot shop at the Santa Cruz Mall, alive
with exotic feathers—we all dressed in colors then—
that woman in the red cape who wandered Mission Blvd.,
street musicians in Guatemalan shirts,
flower shops with tubs of roses by the curb.
Now I'm in snow country, still thinking
of pink and yellow buildings, of persimmons
in the market, and rhododendrons flopping off their stems.
Here, these Eastern woods have just shrugged off winter
and the trees are full of brown birds,
bright voices hiding in the branches.

II

Summers ago in Leland, I watched a swimmer
walk out of Lake Michigan, her wet hair gleaming
and her skin, with its coat of oil,
glittering in the sun. Behind her, blue
and stretching to the sky, the water sparkled.
Everything shone, even crystals of sand around our blanket.
That was the month of butterflies, thousands
of monarchs on their way to Mexico
—I don't know how they can make it so far.
Once, in California, I walked
through the eucalyptus trees at night
and heard the whisper of their wings while they slept.

133

III

When the bear came for me, I already knew
that trees walk at night, that the river speaks,
and the wind knows everything.
It was October, evening at the Yellow Dog. I was
reading near the stove, trying to keep warm, trying
to ignore some mice building a nest on the shelf.
Maybe he was watching all week, maybe
he just found my light—I don't know.
At first I thought his bawling and crying
were embers in the stove, then a cow,
but those Michigan woods were never farmland.
I turned down the lamp and ran to the window and saw
only my own reflection in the light from the fire.

IV

Just weeks ago, I sat on the bank
of the Smith River, up near the Oregon border.
I was mourning snow then, dreaming white hills
and wishing cold wind in the face.
Now, I'm across the country and ice
has just let loose this pond. It's May,
bass shiver up from the mud, and new leaves
reflect on the water's skin. I feel lucky
they've found me, whoever they are
that flow with the water, float on the wind.
At this moment, now, midges and darters skim the surface,
and the bass break in circles to take them.

—Saratoga Springs, New York

Raining All Across the Country

Our words, drifting back and forth over the phone wire,
testify to something: At least we can share this rain.
It marries us again, as if the Sierras, the desert, the Rockies,
the plains, the Mississippi, the Great Lakes
did not separate us—for they are also in rain.
You tell me you have lit a fire. I, also, am chilled
inside my new, thick sweater. The rain falls softly
as my morning slides into your afternoon, and your voice,
through the receiver, moves the small bones of my ear,
then flows like blood to my arms, my legs.

I want to tell you how it is with me—that I am
here in California, yet also there where you are, like an inhale
and exhale, a coming and going that disturbs nothing.
I see you sitting in that green chair, the phone
to your right ear. You are fiddling with something,
a small piece of paper, rolling it into a ball.
Now you stand in front of the desk. You are watching
rain fall on the sumac, on their drenched purple crests,
on their leaves turned to burgundy, on the wet meadow,
on the heavy pine boughs by the hill—all in misty rain.

If I told you this, would you understand? For you,
my rented house is only a number on an envelope. We no longer
share a bed. Your shirts don't hang in my closet. You've never
stood at this window or sat in this borrowed rocker
looking down at this puddled street, these shiny rooftops
slanting down to the bottoms, the foggy bay beyond.
You didn't see me this rainy morning, digging holes
for the daffodil bulbs. When I set them in the earth, I was
placing myself here in spring, in the sunshine that's coming.

—Arcata, California

Christine, On Her Way to China: An Earthquake Poem

"Buy that blouse," she whispered,
the earth already moving, though we didn't know it yet.
We walked over from the car, the blouse
expensive, pulling us to the window.
We walked rich and daring, with that thrust to our hips.

The gold beads were electric; she was my friend.
The night before, when I confessed my sins,
we'd both wept for what might have been—
the dreams that never rose, the lost father of the child in us.
"Buy it," she said in her throaty Austrian way.

She'd just come from snow country to gape at fuchsias,
Scotch broom and poppies by the roadside,
to Northern California where everything grows big and wet and lush.
She'd come from barren white, a nine-month winter,
to trees in leaf and rivers shimmering like snakeskins.

I saw bolts of lightning explode from the black silk;
I felt something break, a sunburst;
I heard a rustle, the crack and fall of timber.
"Aztec goddesses in temples," said Christine.
"Will you take a charge card?" I asked the saleswoman.

The plates were sliding then, the brain exposed,
a flash and spark, granite rasping granite.
The jolt came then, the earth in motion.
Buildings swayed, chimneys fell, the TV talk was rock and grind
    and rumble.
I spun glittering before the mirror and knew we danced the fault.

Christine is flying now to China.
My earthquake blouse gleams from the open closet.
Someone told me once how he'd been standing in a valley,
felt the tremble, and watched the fields roll like ocean waves.

I thought, even then, how we are planted here,
how ordinary our lives are, how we must
make adventure from these briefest shifts and passings.

—Eureka, California

New Poems

Once the way is internalized, practice can be continued anywhere.

—*Zentatsu Baker-Roshi*

Alone at Prairie Creek

In the meadow, the grasses
bend their heads as if in greeting.
Dew glistens and the bench
at the edge of these weeping trees is damp.
This morning, between prairie and forest,
anything is possible.
Last fall, in the dry season, I drank
from a Coke can on this same bench.
A hummingbird, attracted to what I held,
came as far as my hand. I was glad
for that darting visit, though I'd come
for elk browsing in the grass.
When my friend, Joseph, was groundskeeper
in a more civilized place, hummingbirds
chased the red handles of pliers in his pocket.
The year I saw Moira Shearer
dance in that film, *Red Shoes*,
I fell in love with what was
feminine in me. Today I'm alone and
a breeze lifts the alders in commotion.
Later, in a dark part of the redwoods,
I'll find the lens cap from Christine's camera
—she lost it months ago, but things
have a way of appearing suddenly.
It will be where we stood gaping up
at those tallest trees, the tender parts
of our necks exposed, where light
fell through in shafts as if the gods were
looking down, trying to reach us as we prayed.

—Prairie Creek, California

Walking the Riverbed to Wilder Ranch to Watch the Sunset With Joseph and Linden

November, and this California river
runs dry, just dust and rock
in the dark heart of woods. This is the year
I've turned my back on winter:
cold pinching the skin, bear with snow on his shoulders,
house closed and no heat within.

We walk the bank till the brush gets too thick,
then the bed itself, the rough and tumbled spine.
Past sandy bend and rise, sharp descent through granite.
If there were water now, we'd be
below the surface, adrift and nudging the edge,
then rushing this cut to the rapids.

In a month, when ice locks in what I've left
and December's terrible mourning begins,
the moss on these boulders will wave into motion,
these grottos will open, hold secrets again.
This floor will be full of darters and swimmers, this canyon
will din with the echo of falling.

But tonight we'll retrace our steps in the dark. We'll be
blind mice heading home. We'll stumble and grope,
form a line and hold hands,
we'll beg our feet to find the way. We'll say,
"Remember how you came here.
Be like water now, churning down from these hills."

—Santa Cruz, California

142

Brunch at David's in a Storm

—for David Boxer

That green line far out to the horizon—a pause
between these storms rolling into us, over us, one
after the other. Gulls huddle below in the cove,
grounded, and waves explode against the rocks.
Here, by the deck, the wind hits full force.
Rain whips by the window, alders
shake loose their leaves and the fuchsia trembles.
Thorny necks of the roses are battered bare.

We feel it and we don't, insulated high on this cliff.
The ocean is our view, the curving coastline, as if
it's another art object in this well-appointed house.
Inside, we're eating bagels and cream cheese,
smoked albacore and California avacado.
A classical guitar strums through the
stereo speaker. You pause
from cooking that colossal Spanish omelet
to pour more champagne. It's Sunday, this is brunch.
We know how to act—we've learned manners, we've
read hundreds of books. We teach English now.

If our immigrant parents could see us—me sitting here
in my second-hand clothes, you the tireless host,
all that violence rushing by outside.
Nothing is really ours—not this elegant beach house
you rent for the winter, or that Victorian further inland
where I am custodian of furniture.

—Trinidad, California

143

The Language of Whales

Car wipers clearing a path through mist,
I come to where the beached whale
lies rotting at the shoreline.
Last night it was the strum of harps.
Before that, cellos. Today, a chorus singing.
Past a barrier of rock and shallows,
beyond the roll and curl of surf,
they rise and fall, they call him home.

All winter I waited at my window,
walked the cliff for the miracle of seeing
spout or breech or trail of bubbles.
I imagined their bodies light as clouds
gliding over, slipping under, each other.
Last year, from a boat, I watched
three cross our bow—eye and back, then fluke.
I heard them sigh as they breathed in air.

Once, at the Ocean Grove Bar, I met
an old whaler mourning his youth.
"We'd get between the calf and cow
and spear the youngster first," he said.
"The mother was easy after that."
—Don't stop here, don't climb the dune, don't look
at that obscene word someone carved in his flesh.
"Come," they sing across the waves.

When my Cherokee friend was a boy in Oklahoma
a whale was hauled through on a train.
He remembers the crowd at the station, his mother
holding his hand, the dust on his shoes,
the summer heat, the huge shadow
like a felled tree on the flatbed.
He remembers the voices calling—all that way.

—McKinleyville, California

144

California Quail

There they are, in my neighbor's yard,
poking through the ice plants at the fence:
black goatees, white straps, ridiculous
plumes on their soldiers' helmets.
Last week, in the woods at Patrick's Point,
they rustled so in the blackberry bushes
I thought it was a bear
and sang myself a song of courage.

Now it's Monday morning. There's no wind, the ocean's
just a ripple. The neighbor boy's talking to himself
as usual as he readies his bike for school.
Now his spokes flash down the drive, now
the regiment's in front of him.
—He grinds to a halt.

"Quail," I hear his eight-year-old voice.
The birds break formation
and skitter ahead on the gravel.
I hold my breath, wondering.
—At last he remembers his purpose in life
and angles across my lawn.
In line again, the quail march up the drive,
their leader pip-pipping them to order.
What's left is a bicycle track through the dewy grass.

—Trinidad, California

Starlings

When I lived along the coast, starlings filled my lawn.
Shrieking, the black cloud descended,
then lifted as if to shake loose a frenzy,
then lit again to pierce the soil.
They bickered and pecked in a wildness magnified by numbers, then
glinting sparks, they rose,
swarmed sideways to my neighbor's yard,
rapacious voices never ceasing, no time left for breath.
—Only in their absence did I learn to love that darkness.

Visiting the Dead

—for Leslie—La Union, New Mexico

On this clear, New Mexican day, I walk with Leslie
past the corral and her two horses who wait patiently at the fence
for their loved one to come with oats, past the neighbor's llamas
in their stalls, where I'm careful to not get too close, just close enough
to see their cleft lips, the way they chew side to side,
that their hooves are split and divided too.
The neighbor isn't home, but we climb her porch steps anyway
to peer through her window, framed with yellow curtains, at the Navaho rug
on her living room wall, the pueblo pottery on her mantle, the sculpture
of a woman bathing that she, herself, chipped from pink granite.
We walk past the dry irrigation ditch and tumbleweed
caterwauling along the two-track that's coated with tamped-down
cotton blown off the field, our shoes leaving puffs of dust behind us.
We walk the stretch of sand and dirt, heat waves shimmering
against the blue of sky, past scrub brush and strayed, empty
cigarette packs and pieces of wind-fingered paper with the words washed away,
past beer cans, and broken glass glinting silver in the sun,
past stubble and stem, toward the graveyard at the edge of town that moves
closer with our steps, our slow talk, the heat pressing its hand to our backs.
We walk through the gully, then up and out of the ditch, past a yellow dog
panting in the center of the dirt-paved street. We follow the high iron fence
around a corner, our words soft and measured as our steps,
and we enter the gate to this land of the dead, no grass, no water,
a few wilting trees. We climb the dirt slope to carved wooden crosses,
plastic flowers set in jars. Hernandez. Dias. Carillo.
We stop before painted fences that separate families, red or blue, white.
Jimenez. Ortiz. —Iron rails, like the sides of cribs, painted pink and purple.
Gonzalez. Bright flowers on green stems. They lie sleeping in their beds.
We walk home through the dusty town, cactus growing in the yards
of pink houses, blue houses, with black iron doors, bars over windows.
We walk past the dozing dog, past a boy on a rusty bicycle,
and out to the field, to the scrub, to the two-track, the tumbleweed.
We head back to the horses still waiting at the fence.

Snow Geese Over Lincoln, Nebraska

All evening, they pass and keep on passing overhead,
a delirium of voices calling. Over this town
pressed into prairie, over snow
dingy in mounds along curbs and sidewalks,
their chatter goes on and on on the wind.
I've come from further East, not from this flyway,
the ground I've left is still wedded to winter.
I'm headed West into rain. I'm not prepared
for this stirring, this language of longing,
these invisible wings beating North to the tundra.

After dinner, my friend and I walk her neighborhood:
curved streets, landscaped yards, little ranch houses.
We see through picture windows to empty front rooms
—lamps lit at sofa ends, but no one sitting there—
and we wonder: is all of America asleep?
Perhaps the earth has stopped, perhaps she and I are suspended,
alone on this street, and only the wind and the voices are moving.
There's a half moon, stars cluster the sky.
It's cold, a blizzard blew through here a week ago.
We're wearing coats and gloves, scarves at our throats,
and the wind takes our breath when we speak.

Yet even through earmuffs we hear them,
insistent, demanding, calling back and forth in a frenzy.
At the corner, we peer above chimneys and treetops.
They circle our heads, but the night's without end
and we're tied to this earth—left gawking, looking up.
At last they light the sky and they're fireflies flickering.
No—they're snowflakes swirling. No—ghosts trailing shrouds.
They're buffeted this way and that.
They swirl white. They vanish. We find them again.
They're angels sending messages. They're a galaxy,
a milky way spinning off. They're singing hymns to the earth.
They're drifting away. They're leaving us behind. Their song is
Desire. Desire. Desire.

Flying

1.
A boy, poised on his skateboard
at the top of the hill.
This is my street, the descent
to the beach. I've just finished breakfast.
I'm sitting at a round table, looking out
at the ocean, at two surfers
waiting for the right wave. I've been waiting
for whales to pass, spouting on their way back from Baja.
The boy has not yet decided if he will
touch his toe to the pavement and push off,
if he will fly down the hill.

2.
You know the story:
They both board the plane in Chicago.
He's wearing a business suit,
striped shirt, blue tie flecked with red diamonds.
Her hair drifts over her shoulders, her skirt
grazes her knees. In his seat, he recalls
the scent of her perfume.
Over Denver, she pauses at his row.
He follows her up the aisle
—aft, past the galley. They both
return to their seats somewhere
around Salt Lake City. No one
remarks on their absence.

3.

Another boy. This one leaping rocks
with his friend on the edge of Las Cruces.
He's nine and skinny, not as strong,
not as old, as the other one.
It's hot. His hair falls over his forehead,
he clenches his fists and tries to keep up.
He stumbles, but doesn't fall.
The rocks are like cliffs. The spaces
in between are open jaws.
This time, he misjudges and slips,
keeps on sliding, feet first, arms over his head,
down, into the "V" of a crevice.
All day, the medics and police try to pull him up.
They tie ropes to his wrists, but he's stuck
like a swollen tongue in that mouth.
At last, a woman brings salad oil from the grocer's.
They drizzle it onto him. Golden and gooey, it oozes
over his head, down his back. It clings like glue.
They pull. He stretches long. They keep on pulling
until the rocks give him back. There he is—
floating clear, shining in the New Mexico sun.

4.

The mountain climber comes down from his hut
in August. He's been living with hawks, leaping
over boulders and lichen, following thin whispers of trails.
Now he has appointments in the city.
He is lonely in this blare and clang.
The streets are straight and unforgiving, his feet hurt.
He notices the flatness of sidewalks and he nearly
loses his balance at the right angle of a curb.
How embarrassing, he thinks, to spread out
these arms, to be afraid of falling.

150

5.

When Challenger left its plume across the sky,
I was living in California. I had the TV on and was
combing my hair, getting ready for school.
It was January, rainy season on the west coast,
but in Florida the sky was cloudless.
All week, gale winds and rain kept beating against my window
while Challenger exploded again and again on TV.
Fragments scattering in the air,
white trails skittering against a blue backdrop.
Christa McAuliffe was a civilian, a schoolteacher,
she planned to send lessons from the shuttle
to students in Concord, New Hampshire.
How will we measure the depth of blue in oceans or sky?
Where does space end and heaven begin?
When do angels become invisible.

6.

Karl Wallenda was 73 when he agreed to walk the high wire
between two hotels in San Juan. He'd already
looked down at broken pieces of his family
on a circus floor, as if they'd been shot from the sky.
He'd already caught his niece in mid-air
after their pyramid collapsed in Detroit.
"We are not the Flying Wallendas, not trapeze artists,"
he shouted at reporters. "We are sky walkers,
the Great Wallendas. We do not use a net."
In his thin slippers, he has walked across the sky
in stadiums and parks, over gorges, between other hotels.
Now he is 73. He is in Puerto Rico, ten stories up, 120 feet,
he has made a promise and the crowd is waiting.
He steps out of the hotel window, only the balance pole
in his hands, a miniature man to those below.
This morning, there was just a breeze, but now wind
puffs between the buildings. He hesitates, then begins.

A few steps, a pause. Wind lifts his hair.
Now he is mid-way. His shirt balloons, his pant legs flap.
Wind slaps his face. He stops again.
The wire wobbles. He bends to make himself smaller.
"Sit down, Poppi," his granddaughter shouts from below.
When his foot slips, he tries to grab the wire.
All the way down, he holds the balance pole
in perfect sky-walking position.

Sleepwalkers

1.
The bee in its buzz, the moose bellowing:
He spoke and was both of them,
hands outstretched, bare feet
padding down the carpeted hall.
When his robe fell open
the round moon of his belly led the way
—his body disconnected
from the stranger's voice that was his.

2.
One night, in a motel, I dreamed a swan
snagged in a streambed.
When I woke, it was
the actress next door, her headboard
slapping against my wall. I heard
him grunting, her awful cry,
the swan flapping its wings, begging
to be lifted into the air so that it could fly.

3.
In the girl's dream, the bear
wore a winged coat that buttoned down the front.
Her mother pleaded with her to stay, but
the bear's eyes were blue flame
and she ran to him.
When they flew, the girl
did not ride on his back, but under,
close to his heart.

4.
All night, a banging and pounding
has brought this house to its knees.
Workmen on scaffolds and ladders try to
hold up the walls, but something heavy
thunders over the roof. It roars
at the windows, claws at the doors.
Yes, I am afraid, but not of this. —Afraid
of turning, of walking away.

At Manitoulin

The summer I sailed among islands,
rowdy teenagers came to the government wharf
where I'd tied for the night. I shouldn't have been
on reservation land and was afraid
they might cut my lines, set me adrift in the starless dark.
"Please," I called, standing at the open hatchway, "can you
not be so noisy? I'm trying to sleep."
In the silence, eyes of cigarettes glowed.
—At dawn, I gathered empty bottles left against the pilings.

It was noon when the Indian boy came on his pony,
its hooves clattering over the dock's rough timbers.
Neither of them had been this close to a sailboat, and the horse
shied when I came onto the deck.
The boy peered into the cabin for a long time before he
climbed down, then he touched the gimballed stove,
the instruments on the chart table, he trailed his finger
over the fences that held my books in their shelves.

He sat on the edge of a berth and drank juice I poured,
and told how the pony had studied its face
in the dusty window of his grandpa's shed
until it fell in love with its own image. He said
he'd like to go to school on the mainland,
maybe travel to the States when he grew up.
Before I set sail, I gave the horse two carrots,
the boy helped me cast off. When I got to open water,
I looked back at the two of them, standing at the end
of the dock—the boy's arm around the pony's neck,
the pony whispering in his ear.

—North Channel, Canada

155

Recognizing

On M-46, just west of Cedar Springs,
after the Chrysler in front swerved and sped on, I had to brake
for the mallard. Eleven ducklings followed,
so close she looked to be dragging broken feathers.
After they'd crossed and disappeared in tall grass
through a cut in the barbed-wire fence, I smiled at the east-
bound pickup, also stopped. Blond man with a beard:
he grinned and waved. Both of us were shining.

October Light

1. Driving

Driving past blur of fencepost,
past cornstalks bleached and bent,
past fallow field and grasses dying on the shoulder,
lost in the business of highway, of getting
from point to circled map-point, towns
rolling by like old newsreels,
the eye's pupil narrows, won't open
its tiny focus or let the hungry heart expand
until the car rounds a curve, until
the driver pulls off the road
and stops near a pond.
—Here, sun pierces brilliant sky,
weave of color in the hills,
pattern of green and gold and scarlet,
fleck of mauve. Here, blood seeps
down branch and trunk to yellow
already scattered at the edge,
to reflection, to water that
opens its mouth and swallows all this brilliance.

2. In Town—Caledonia, New York

Up Maple Street, over on Elm,
down Locust near the Trinity Union Church,
around corners, near fenceposts,
in sunlight's blaze and leaf-turn,
this town prepares for spirits.
Skeletons leap from parlor windows, pumpkins
spill down drives, witches' brooms
and sheaves of husks stand sentinel at stairs.
On white-washed porches, rag-stuffed aged
accept the wind in chairs that rattle as they rock.

157

This town is old, history was born here
—land was cleared, a war was fought,
gossip stretches back for generations.
At dusk, these robed and melon-headed ghosts,
tied now and hanging from the maples,
will dance and beckon to the cemetery,
calling home the rest of it.

3. Home—New Era, Michigan
Traveling from workplace, from meeting room,
from neighboring town or store or mall,
along roads on fire with sumac and sugar maple,
the heart smolders in a passion of oak.
Past yellow poplar and beech, past trembling birch,
past staccato of black gum by the orchard, past
blaze of blueberry bush and humming meadow grass.
At last, up the winding two-track, key already turned
to unlock the inner life, house inside these golden ash trees,
secret veins and bones of floor and wall and roof.
Climbing the stairs, opening the door, entering
this heat—this light—that leans willingly into winter.

First Snow

I love this meadow with all the weeds erased,
this stunned silence
with no house in sight, everything soft
as chimney smoke, as the breath steaming out of my mouth.
When we were children in the city, we'd count
star-points on snowflakes, then lick them off our mittens.
We loved what was cold then, loved
the feel of change in our bodies.

Now I live in the country, just this old black dog
for a friend, and we're on our way to the mailbox
—it's the same path we've traveled through summer and fall,
only this time our steps creak on fresh-fallen snow.
Past the curve of the drive is the road to town,
but I'm watching the dog prance along beside me,
I'm listening to chickadees in the pine tree in the hollow,
I'm counting all the blizzards and thaws I've spent here.

The dog stops to sniff where a rabbit has paused
and the world seems poised on its axis.
Coming back, her nose will record that we've passed here,
I'll be holding white envelopes with their own trail to follow.
—But now, we're here. We haven't reached the road.
Now the chickadees explode from the pine in a clamor
and the dog turns to me and she looks like she's grinning.
Now she throws herself down on the snow, she rolls
onto her back, she spreads out her wings.
I think I see ghosts in the birch grove up the hill.
I'm talking to my dear ones in heaven.

—New Era, Michigan

Deer at the Door

What drew them up the hill, away
from sheltering pines, overgrown sumac, everything
in leaf now that summer's nearly here?
Was it light inside this little house,
our soft conversation, our attention
to the roast, the salad, before us?
What is it they saw, standing by the window,
their gentle heads raised, then browsing
again in the grass? Was it our shadows
bent over our plates, our acceptance
of what we have, what we are,
as the slow weight of day began to leave?
—I remember the beginning of a moment:
the sparrow's throat opening, the dog
rising from her place on the rug, me standing, you
looking up, the song starting, the dog and I
crossing the room, my hand on the door,
the smiles on our faces, the song on its last notes,
everything in harmony for a few beats of the heart.
Then the door opened
and their heads lifted, the air turned still.
I heard the rustle of grass, saw their white tails flash
as they darted awkwardly down the hill,
and dusk came on like the closing of an eye.

—New Era, Michigan

160

Walking the Beach in Fog

In this blind world, lost
between sunrise and evening, the dog and I
follow the shoreline north.
No tourists will come here today.
The dunes have disappeared and the horizon,
the sky, the driftwood logs and ore boats.
We exist in only a circle of light.
The dog stays within range of my voice—
we don't want to lose each other.
Muted, without color, we're dots
on a fractured piece of landscape
where even the water has lost all blue:
If we were a painting, we'd be
"Black Dog and Woman in White," nameless,
suspended, viewed by no one, walking nowhere.
Ahead and behind swirls another world and I think
of that winter I skied in Switzerland
when we were caught in clouds coming down the mountain,
when I was young, when I lost
my sense of up and down and thought I was floating.
We groped our way then, cautious ghosts
traversing the trail. With each turn on the descent,
we had to bend low, touch the snow, make sure
it was under us. Today there's just the dog and me,
whatever waits ahead remains unseen.
Even these deer tracks fade to nothing. If I
walk deeper into this fog, the dog may not follow me
and if she doesn't, what will know me there?

—New Era, Michigan

161

Destroying the Cormorant Eggs

Black, black as the plumage
of the double-crested cormorant, all black
except for the orange chin pouch below its slender,
curved bill, who nests by the shore in shadow and crack
of rock along with the lighter, tan or gray or white
gulls and terns on Little Gull Island and Gravelly Island
in the middle of Lake Michigan— Black as the long shadow
of this fisherman, or madman, slipping
over these rocks, these nests, an eclipse or is it God,
some thing without conscience between sun and earth/water,
his staff much like a shepherd's crook, but
this time carried for balance and for the rest of it: the
choosing, knowing which eggs, only lovely pale blue,
not the gulls' and terns' brown or buff, then
to lift out, to hurl against the granite,
to punish them for fishing these waters,
to crush under boot or beat with his stick,
2000 eggs, the cormorants now emitting faint squawks,
flapping their wings over this darkness,
the albumin and yolk, the embryos shining on dull rock,
the small pieces of sky fallen down—Black
as the night waters of a man's dream where he gropes
below the surface, groaning with the old hungers,
the luminescence of his skin covered by something
so thick his arms stroke heavy with it, the water
without end, and no island, no island in sight.

The Beach Stairs

1.
Last week, on the cliff, the air
hung humid, but sun
beamed through the cedars.
As I descended,
the beach disappeared,
—fog blending sky and earth, folding itself
over the lake's secrets.

2.
Once, I spied on a walking stick,
ancient teacher picking his way
along the underside of this railing.
Another time, I startled
a fawn sunning on the landing.
I am always the intruder
when I enter their world.

3.
That hawk ahead of me keeps leaving its perch.
As I walk the water's edge
it bustles the air
—pine tree to snag to leafy limb.
My footsteps steady,
shadow following,
I had no intention of heading south today.

4.

The school of fish traveling north
out past the second sandbar
resembles porpoises leaping,
but they don't disturb those gulls
floating above them.

5.

The water so clear today
I can see hundreds of minnows close to shore.
Years ago, when we camped at Ludington,
I learned to seine them with a towel.
The few my brother and I captured
we saved in sand pails, but our mother
never let us bring them back to the trailer.

6.

Here is the small spit
that joins shore to first sandbar.
Here is the pool between them.
Here is the old black dog,
dead three years now,
leaping off the bar
into the sun-warmed pool.
Here I am, leaping too.
Laughing and grinning, again
and again, the two of us
leaping and swimming back, leaping again.
—A game between us,
pure and simple.

7.
The mistress of that big poodle
held him until I passed.
"He would give you a wet, joyful
greeting," she solemnly told me.
I didn't say how much I'd been hoping
for exactly that. The dog
pretended sobriety, but I noticed his hilarious tail.

8.
Last month, this Canada goose
led her seven goslings
out of brush along the cliff to the surf.
Tails wagging, little balls of fluff,
the dutiful line tumbled into the water.
Now here they are, full-grown.
Stiff-necked, heads high,
they face the waves and sail off,
serene and unruffled as Victorians on a Sunday stroll.

9.
At the slide, where the spring keeps on
running down its muddy path,
two cardinals take turns
taking their shower in the waterfall.
Just their size, it must have been made for them.

10.
Diane, her first time in Lake Michigan,
first time in ten years in shorts, standing in
knee-deep water at the first sandbar,

laughing and waving her arms like a child,
like she must have done before her brother
killed himself for justice in the Pacific Ocean.

11.
The surf is rough,
but this turtle, its eggs laid, won't quit
trying to return to water.
Westward it crawls, but waves keep tossing it back.
Now on its hard shell, legs swimming the air,
it can't get free. Soon sand will bury it
—so I carry it out past the breakers and let it go.

—The Claybanks/Lake Michigan

Leaving

—a November poem

So still by this spring
that each sound grows
its own body. I watch
a wren of a leaf float
to the pond and my breath
sinks into the water.

On the ridge, pines
swing before the wind
falls down this hill,
before a flock of oak leaves
lets loose its perch,
takes flight over my head.

Walking with the Bear

New snow, and I follow
the dim path through woods, sink
into silence. Meadow vole, squirrel,
snowshoe hare, fox:
my tracks walk next to theirs.
If it still falls tonight, by dawn
none of us have traveled here.

Notes

Every effort has been made to trace copyright holders of quoted material in this book. The author apologizes if any work has been used without permission and would be glad to be told of anyone who has not been consulted.

from *Lake Songs and Other Fears*

Title Page: "Those grand fresh-water seas of ours, —Erie, and Ontario, and Huron, and Superior, and Michigan, . . . they know what shipwrecks are, for out of sight of land, they have drowned full many a midnight ship with all its shrieking crew." Herman Melville, *Moby Dick* (Oxford: Oxford University Press, 1998).

"Leland": "Robert" in this poem is Robert Vas Dias, a British poet who was born and raised in Scotland and lived in Michigan for several years. Leland, a small town on Lake Michigan, is a recognized safe harbor. This poem and "The Fourth of July Drowning" are set there.

"Homage to Mr. Bones": A tribute to John Berryman and his work, written after he jumped off the bridge in Minneapolis. The title is taken from Berryman's 1956 long poem "Homage to Mistress Bradstreet." Mr. Bones and Henry are both Berryman personas and are found in his later poems. Several abbreviated phrases from Berryman's poems are incorporated into this poem with the intention of paying tribute to the master in a "common language." See John Berryman, *Henry's Fate & Other Poems, 1967–1972* (New York: Farrar, Straus, and Giroux, 1977)

from *In the Presence of Mothers*

Title Page: "All of us forever seeking again this warmth and this darkness, this being alive without pain, this being alive without anxiety or fear or aloneness." Anaïs Nin, *The Diary of Anaïs Nin 1931–1934* (New York: Harcourt Brace Jovanovich, Inc.), Reprinted by permission.

"Palmistry for Blind Mariners": This sequence evolved after contemplating the image of the Lower Peninsula of Michigan—that is, that it is shaped like a hand—and from having been a student of palmistry at about the same time.

from Counting the Losses

"I mean . . . the work, and the life, must have their origin in a place of conviction for the poet" John Haines, "Roots," in *Living Off the Country: Essays on Poetry and Place* (Ann Arbor, Mich.: University of Michigan Press, 1981), 85.

"I am not one of those who left the land." Anna Akhmatova, "I Am Not One of Those Who Left the Land . . .," in *Poems of Akhmatova*, trans. Stanley Kunitz and Max Haward (Boston, Mass.: Little, Brown and Co., 1973), 75.

"When I went away from all things, when I left the place / my feet knew, . . . I wanted to cry." Rebecca Newth, "A Journey Whose Bones Are Mine," in *A Journey Whose Bones Are Mine* (St. Paul, Minn.: Truck Press, 1978), 27.

"For there is . . . a genius of place, a presence, and because there is, people's feelings accumulate about it." James Wright, "The Pure Clear Word: An Interview with Dave Smith," in *Collected Prose*, ed. Anne Wright (Ann Arbor, Mich.: University of Michigan Press, 1983), 194.

"We *are* it / it sings through us." Gary Snyder, "By Frazier Creek Falls," in *Turtle Island* (New York: New Directions, 1974), 41.

"We cannot see that invisible winds carry us, as they carry swarms of locusts, that invisible magnetism brings us as it brings the migrating birds." D. H. Lawrence, "The Spirit of Place," in *Studies in Classic American Literature* (New York: Penguin Books, 1923, 1977), 13.

"How else can you live but with the knowledge / of old lives continuing in fading / sepia blood under your feet?" Margaret Atwood, "The Bus to Alliston, Ontario," in *Two-Headed Poems* (Toronto, Ont.: Oxford University Press, 1978), 78.

"When you say, 'I live here,' animals / you hadn't thought of for years live on your lawn. / They insist you remember their names." Richard Hugo, "Houses," in *White Center* (New York: W. W. Norton and Co, 1980), 68.

"In this field, / Where the small animals ran from a brush fire, / It is a voice / In burned weeds, saying / I love you." James Wright, "Brush Fire," in *Collected Poems* (*Shall We Gather at the River*) (Middletown, Conn.: Wesleyan University Press, 1971), 156.

"The female is as it were a deformed male . . . " Aristotle, *Generation of Animals*, trans. A. L. Peck (Cambridge, Mass.: Harvard University Press, 1963), 175. Taken from the notes by Susan Griffin, *Woman and Nature: The Roaring Inside Her*, 1st ed. (New York: Harper & Row, 1978).

"One hundred women are not worth a single testicle." Confucius quoted by Meg Bowman, *Why We Burn: Sexism Exorcised: A Dramatic Reading on Sexism in Religion* (San Jose, Calif.: Hot Flash Press, 1984).

"Blessed art thou, O Lord our God and King of the Universe, that thou didst not create me a woman." Orthodox Jewish prayer quoted by Meg Bowman, *Why We Burn*. See also Simone de Beauvoir, *The Second Sex* (New York: Bantam Books, 1953), xxi.

"Every woman should be overwhelmed with shame at the thought that she is a woman." St. Clement of Alexandria quoted by Meg Bowman, *Why We Burn*.

Women were "castrated men" "penis envy." Sigmund Freud, *The Freud Reader* (New York: W. W. Norton & Co. Inc., 1989), 665. See also Germaine Greer, *Female Eunuch* (New York: McGraw-Hill, 1971).

"a fair defect / of Nature" John Milton, *John Milton's Paradise Lost*, ed. Harold Bloom (New York: Chelsea House, 1996).

"It is almost a pity a woman has a womb." Anonymous 19th century physician quoted in *The Female Hero: An Anthology of Literary Texts on Women's Quest*, ed. Lene Lundsgaard and Nina Nørgaard (Copenhagen: Scriptor, 1985), 19.

"I don't look at myself as a commodity, but I'm sure a lot of people have." Marilyn Monroe quoted in *Life*. From Alicia Ostriker, *Writing Like a Woman* (Ann Arbor, Mich: University of Michigan Press, 1983), 140.

"Man for the field and woman for the hearth . . . / man to command, and woman to obey." Alfred Lord Tennyson, "The Princess," in *Tennyson's Poetry*, ed. Robert W. Hill, Jr. (New York: W. W. Norton & Co. Inc., 1971), 130–203.

"the damned mob of scribbling women" and their "trash." Nathaniel Hawthorne, *Hawthorne and His Publisher* (Port Washington, N.Y.: Kennikat Press, 1969), 14. See also Emily Stipes Watts, ed., *The Poetry of American Women from 1632–1945* (Austin: University of Texas Press, 1977), 68.

"What we admire in woman, / Is her affection, not her intellect." Henry Wadsworth Longfellow quoted in Watts, *Poetry of American Women*, 71.

"(Women) weren't born to be free, they were born to have babies." Norman Mailer, *Deer Park* (New York: Perigee Books, 1981). See also Lundsgaard and Nørgaard, eds., *The Female Hero*.

"If I wish to define myself, I must first of all say: 'I am a woman'; . . . a man never begins by presenting himself as an individual of a certain sex." de Beauvoir, "Introduction," *The Second Sex*, xvii.

"and if . . . a white sweating bull of a poet told us / our cunts are ugly—why didn't we / admit we have thought so too?" Denise Levertov, "Hypocrite Woman," in *O Taste and See* (New York: New Directions, 1964), 70.

"Death? Why this fuss about death. Use your imagination, try to visualize a world *without* death." Charlotte Perkins Gilman, from *The Living of Charlotte Perkins Gilman* quoted in Elaine Partnow, ed., *The Quotable Woman*, vol. I (Los Angeles, Calif.: Pinnacle, 1977, 1980), 270.

"Death and labour are things of necessity and not of choice." Simone Weil, "Part III," from *The Need for Roots* quoted in Partnow, *The Quotable Woman*, vol. II, 147.

"Life has got to be lived. That's all there is to it." Eleanor Roosevelt, from *The New York Times*, 8 October 1954, quoted in Elaine Partnow, ed., *The Quotable Woman*, vol. I (Los Angeles, Calif.: Pinnacle, 1977, 1980), 270, 472.

"Life's under no obligation to give us what we expect. We take what we get and are thankful it's no worse than it is." Margaret Mitchell, "Part V, Ch. 53," from *Gone With the Wind*, quoted in Partnow, *The Quotable Woman*, vol. II, 21.

"I am afraid of dying—but being dead, oh yes, that to me is often an appealing prospect." Kathe Kollwitz, "December, 1941," from *Diaries and Letters*, quoted in Partnow, *The Quotable Woman*, vol. I, 10.

"The years seem to rush by now, and I think of death as a fast-approaching end of a journey—double and treble reason for loving as well as working while it is day." George Eliot, "Letter to Miss Sara Hennell, Nov. 22, 1861," from *George Eliot's Life as Related in Her Letters and Journals*, quoted in Partnow, *The Quotable Woman*, vol. I, 90.

"I contemplate death as though I were continuing after its arrival." Pearl Buck, "Part I," from *The Goddess Abides* quoted in Partnow, *The Quotable Woman, vol. I*, 562.

"They have made of their lives a great adventure." Ruth Benedict. "January, 1917" Quoted in Margaret Mead, ed., *An Anthropologist at Work: Writings of Ruth Benedict* (Westport, Conn.: Greenwood Press, 1951). See also Partnow, *The Quotable Woman, vol. I*, 502.

"You need only claim the events of your life to make yourself yours." Florida Scott-Maxwell, *The Measure of My Days*, 1972. See also Partnow, *The Quotable Woman, vol. I*, 463.

"If I had it to do again, I would travel lighter than I have . . . I would start barefoot earlier in the Spring. . . I would go to more dances . . . ride more merry-go-rounds. I would pick more daisies." Nadine Stair, "If I Had My Life to Live Over . . . ," *If I Had My Life to Live Over . . .* (Watsonville, Calif.: Papier-Mache Press, 1992).

from *Dancing the Fault*

"A Sense of Place": "There is a genius of place, a presence, and because there is, people's feelings accumulate about it." James Wright, "The Pure Clear Word," *Collected Prose* (Ann Arbor, Mich.: University of Michigan Press, 1983). Reprinted by permission.

"Six Poems for Nine Crows": In the summer and fall of 1979, a group of Mohawk Indian people at Akwesasne (St. Regis Reservation) were under repeated threat of armed assault by a New York State Olympic SWAT team over the issue of the Mohawks' refusal to allow unlawful arrest warrants to be served on members of their community. A particularly tense situation developed after the confiscation by a Mohawk elder of two chain saws and a brush hog from trespassers who were destroying his property.

from *"New Poems"*

Title Page: "Once the way is internalized, practice can be continued anywhere." Zentatsu Baker Roshi (verbal) Used by permission.